MOTO GP
Yesterday & Today

This is a Carlton Book

First published in 2011
This edition published by Carlton Books in 2014
20 Mortimer Street, London, W1T 3JW

10 9 8 7 6 5 4 3 2 1

A CIP catalogue record for this book is available from the British Library.

ISBN 13: 978-1-78097-605-1

Art Direction: Luke Griffin
Designer: Ben Ruocco
Production: Maria Petalidou
Picture Research: Paul Langan
Editorial: Jane Donovan
Project Editor: Matthew Lowing

Printed in China

MOTO GP
Yesterday & Today

Michael Scott

CARLTON
BOOKS

Contents

Foreword: 5

Introduction: 7

One: The Riders 8

Two: The Machines 58

Three: The Track 90

Four: The People 130

Five: The Racing 164

Foreword by Valentino Rossi

I love the history of racing, and I am grateful and proud to be part of it.

I love the way *Moto GP Yesterday & Today* contrasts the early days and the pioneer Grand Prix heroes with racing today.

It all seems so different: the bikes, the speeds, the professionalism. We've come a very long way since the first championship in 1949.

In some ways, it's so much better. Especially safety. Thanks to all those people who have worked for that: we're still working on it today.

Among all the changes one thing has stayed the same: the spirit of racing. The desire – the need to win that drives us all: past generations, current riders and racers of the future.

It may only be numbers, but I have always recognized the milestones in my career, especially race wins. I marked with respect when I passed Mike Hailwood's total of 76 and celebrated with Angel Nieto when I passed his total of 90. As I write, I have 106: Giacomo Agostini has 122, but I am still going. First place is in my sights.

Right: Giants on the grid — a rare photograph of 1950s stars lining up for the West German GP at the Nürburgring in 1955. In pole position nearest the camera, Geoff Duke's Gilera is alongside the works BMWs of Walter Zeller and John Surtees, in a one-off race for the German factory.

Introduction

Don't they look quaint, those old bikes of the 1950s – spindly wire wheels and skinny tyres; bulbous bodywork. And hardly leaning round the corner compared to the 60-degree elbow-scrapers of today.

And the riders, in their pudding-basin helmets, wearing jackets and ties when not on their machines.

It's easy to feel patronizing when you look back at the past. Easy, but badly wrong. As is abundantly clear when you study the images on the pages that follow. Juxtapose old with new, and it is the similarities as much as the differences that command the imagination.

This is not a history book, but it is about history. One that began, strictly speaking, four decades before the foundation of the World Championship in 1949. History that is still being made.

Motorcycling has its own special breed of superstars: Duke, Hailwood, Agostini, Rossi, to name but four. The World Championship series is remarkable also for those out of the limelight. Slower riders. The smaller classes. Mechanics. Girlfriends. The media. The camp followers of racing over all the years. All celebrated in this book.

In every respect they have become much more numerous over the decades, except for the riders. The first premier-class championship race, the Isle of Man Senior TT, had 59 starters. Most of the other five inaugural races of 1949 had more than 30. In 2014, Moto GP numbers were just 24. It had become a more exclusive club.

Of course the machines have changed radically. A top-level 500 of 1949 was proud to manage more than 50 horsepower. The third-generation 1000cc Moto GP machines, festooned in electronics, multiplied that by more than five.

But the basic control equation and the rider's feel are the same, but for the migration of the gear lever from British right to Continental left. Grand Prix motorcycles still go round corners the same way, too – on the edge of the tyre grip, leaning as far as physics allow.

The biggest changes have come in management, professionalism and presentation. Financial stability has brought a security that privateers never knew in the early years … they would sometimes travel to distant circuits without being sure they had an entry.

The most important progress is in safety. Regular deaths were expected in racing when the Championship began. It took many years before people began to realize that it need not be so. Nowadays vastly improved protection – helmets and leathers, and trackside safety means fatalities are very rare.

Some things are better now. Some things are worse.

The pictures that follow will help you decide which are which.

Michael Scott, 2014

One

The Riders

Right: Grand Prix stars at Brands Hatch for the international Race of the South in 1969. Yamaha team-mates/rivals Phil Read (5) and Bill Ivy lead Giacomo Agostini's MV Agusta. Mike Hailwood (3) rode the retired-from-racing 297cc Honda Six and won.

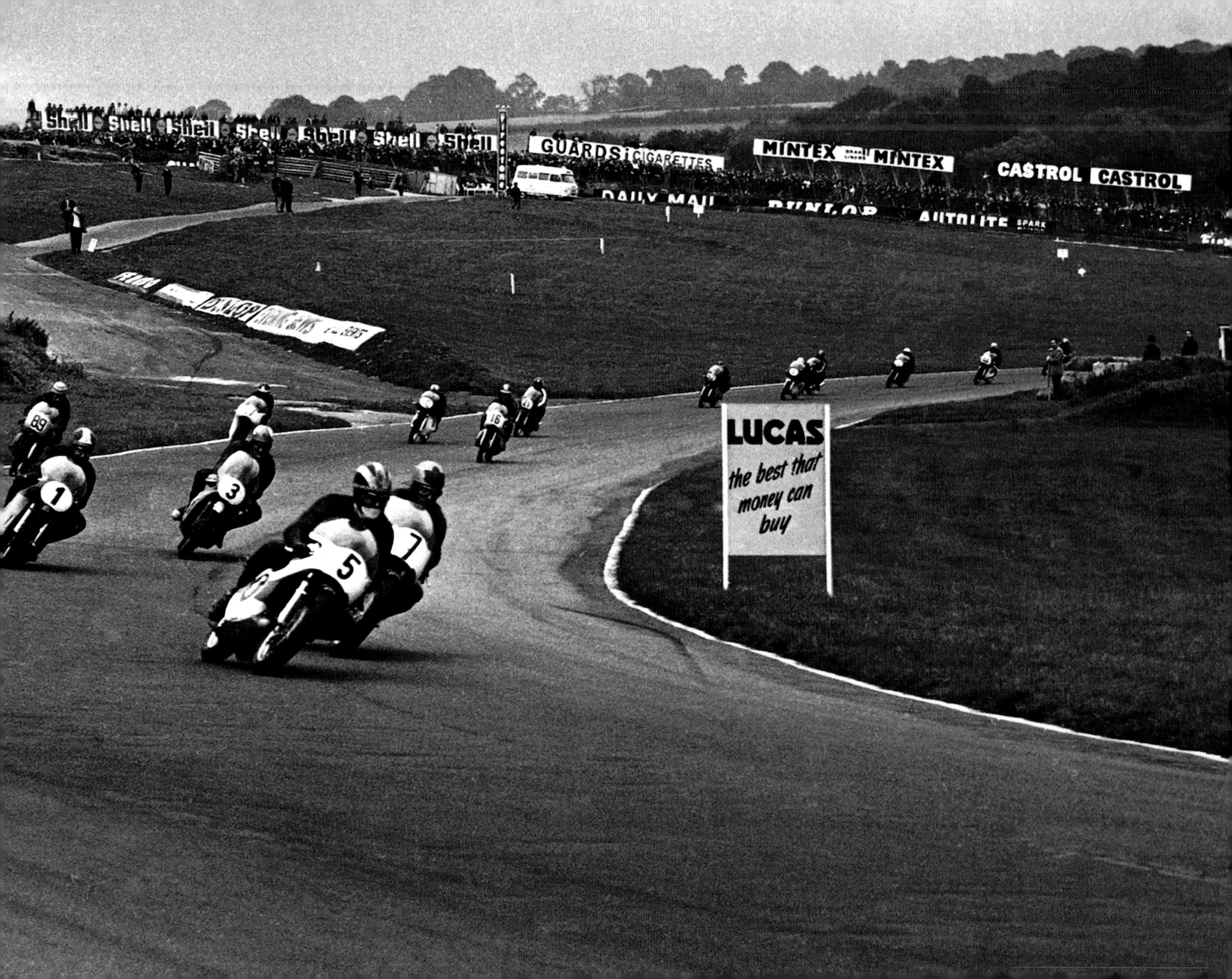
Shell
GUARDS CIGARETTES
MINTEX
CASTROL
DAILY MAIL
DUNLOP
AUTOLITE
LUCAS
the best that money can buy

1974

Great Champions

MOTORCYCLE RACING'S MOUNT RUSHMORE has some distinct and instantly recognizable profiles: the jutting jaw of Mike Hailwood; the chiselled features of Giacomo Agostini; Kenny Roberts – small and fierce; Mick Doohan with his distant stare; the cheeky grin of Valentino Rossi. Trouble is, there are so many others jostling for space.

Like solemn-faced John Surtees, who won five titles then quit bikes for Formula One at the height of his powers. He was irked by factory MV Agusta restrictions that confined him to international races only; he wanted to race every weekend. Surtees went on to become F1 World Champion as well, the only man to achieve the ultimate honour on both two and four wheels. (Although pre-war ace Tazio Nuvolari had done the same before the championships had been instituted.)

Like Wayne Rainey, fighting back for a straight fourth 500 crown when a spine-snapping crash ended his career in 1993. Or tough little Spaniard Angel Nieto, whose 13 World Championships were in 50 and 125cc classes, but who still lies second in terms of titles to Agostini, supreme with 15. Rossi has nine, equal with Mike Hailwood and 125/250 specialist Carlo Ubbiali from Italy.

Or one could count race wins. In all classes, Rossi on 106 is chasing Ago's 122, having outstripped Nieto (90), Hailwood (76) and Doohan (54). And the greatest of all? There's no answer. They were the greatest of their time. If they were to race each other today, I'd back Mike Hailwood.

Left: Lucky 13 – Giacomo Agostini, after winning the Daytona 200 in 1974, following his headline move to Yamaha from MV Agusta. He won his 13th championship in 1975.

Right: Italian pedigree – like Agostini, Valentino Rossi is champion in multiple classes. Now he's chasing his total of wins.

1975

The Nearly Men

SOMETIMES COMING SECOND MIGHT be an honourable result. In a harsher modern era, second is just "the first loser". And for every winner, there must be a whole field of them.

For some riders, simply reaching Grand Prix level is enough in itself. They have no expectation of winning and are satisfied just to take part. Others are thwarted by a variety of reasons that do not necessarily include a shortage of talent. More is needed to be a winner, especially a serial winner ... the right machine, the right tyres and the right luck to escape serious injury in the inevitable occasional crash.

Losing hurts most when you are beaten by your own team-mate, riding a bike the same as yours. It's bad enough when it's by team orders – Bill Ivy is famous for stopping by the track at the 1968 Isle of Man TT after setting a sensational 100mph 125cc lap record, so everyone could see he was letting Yamaha team-mate Phil Read win. Worse still for Shinya Nakano, who lost the 250 title to Yamaha team-mate Olivier Jacque in 2000 by inches, when he was outfumbled on the run to the flag.

Left: The biggest talent never to win a championship: Randy Mamola was four times runner-up, and twice third. His problem was the level of Golden Age talent between 1980 and 1987.

Opposite: Perennial top privateer Jack Findlay. The Australian's career spanned almost 20 years, and he was six times in the championship top five.

1954

Old Hands and Young Guns

GRAND PRIX RACERS SELDOM RETIRE due to old age, but many of them have continued into their forties, particularly in the early years.

The first series of 1949 was won, in the premier class, by a seasoned 37-year-old, shortly to turn 38. That was Les Graham, still the oldest man to win the top prize. But like many of his rivals, the popular AJS-mounted Englishman had raced internationally before the 1939–45 World War Two and was resuming an interrupted career. In the meantime, he had been decorated for bravery as an RAF bomber pilot.

Today's Grand Prix winners are chasing youngest-ever records. They have the advantage of a minimum age of 15 for the 125 class and in the way of modern sports, most have started their careers by the age of 10. Graham is not the oldest World Champion, however. That was German Hermann Paul (H-P, or "Happy") Müller on a factory NSU, who took the 250 title in 1955, aged 45 years and 287 days.

The youngest champion in any class is the recently retired Loris Capirossi, 1990 125 champion, aged 17 and 165 days. The feisty little Italian raced on until 2011, aged 38, with two more titles and 29 all-class GP wins.

The youngest premier-class champion is Marc Marquez, in 2013, aged 20 and 266 days, displacing 1983 champion Freddie Spencer by eight days short of a full year.

And the youngest-ever race winner? That's Briton Scott Redding, who won his home 125 GP in 2008, at 15 years and 170 days, too young to taste the champagne on the podium. A higher minimum age of 16 means his record will stand for the foreseeable future.

Left: Aged 42 and yet to retire, Nello Pagani won races for Gilera in 1949, and was still racing (for MV Agusta) at the Dutch TT in 1954.

Opposite: Old enough to spray champagne, too young to drink it. Scott Redding, aged 15, became youngest-ever GP winner in Britain in 2008, defeating eventual champion Mike di Meglio (left). His record will stand until the rules are changed again.

1953

Fit to Drive

MOTORCYCLE RACING IS AN ATHLETIC BUSINESS. During the 40-odd minutes of a race, total mental concentration is matched by physical effort. It's more than a matter of just hanging on, though that can be hard enough.

The strain peaks under braking, when a rider's arms have to sustain a full 2G of deceleration at the same time as manipulating the hand controls – although nowadays a computer takes care of blipping the throttle on down-shifts.

Every advance in tyre adhesion increases this load and the amount of effort fed into the handlebars, especially in quick changes of direction.

Steering is accomplished by the rider shifting his body, weighting one footpeg or other, using the angle to increase front or rear grip or to promote a wheelspinning slide.

No wonder modern riders in the premier class all follow a gruelling programme of fitness, whether it be long-distance cycling, gym work or running (usually a combination of all three).

Some take it to extremes: Manuel Poggiali, 125 and 250 champion in the early 2000s, took a set of scales to the table and carefully weighed out the ingredients of his balanced breakfast.

Triple 500 champion Wayne Rainey used to run for 10 or 15 miles a day, sometimes more, in the run-up to a new season in the early 1990s. He devised his own method of keeping going. "I'd just imagine Kevin Schwantz running a little ahead of me and I'd try and catch him up."

Left: Rhodesian Ray Amm calms his nerves with a filter-tip before mounting his Norton for the Dutch TT at Assen in 1953.

Right: "The knee-bone's connected to the shoulder-bone; the ankle bone's connected to the hip bone, now shake dem skeleton bones." Rossi enacts a variation on the old song as part of his pre-race stretching ritual.

1965

Getting On

BEST OF FRIENDS OFF THE TRACK, deadly rivals on it? The cliché doesn't hold too much water. Friendships are fragile in racing, for all sorts of reasons.

In more dangerous times riders would avoid becoming close because of the regular fatalities. It was easier to keep your distance. And friendships would be strained by racing circumstances.

Phil Read and Bill Ivy were close ... until they were battling for the championship, and Phil beat Bill in defiance of Yamaha team orders.

Phil Read and Barry Sheene used to party together too ... until an incident when Phil asked for Barry's help in a race to allow him to win the 1975 title. Barry alleged attempted bribery, though Read denied it. But the outcome was undisputed. "We became un-friends," as Read later put it.

The best friendships are between riders racing in different classes. Marco Melandri recalls happy times at home in Italy with Valentino Rossi, when Melandri was one class lower. "It ended when I started to race him close in MotoGP," said Melandri.

But there are exceptions. Kevin Schwantz and Daryl Beattie were team-mates (that most strained of relationships) at Suzuki in 1995, but partied and even went on a hunting safari together. For the record, Beattie never did challenge Schwantz seriously for the title.

Left: Post-race pals: third-placed Giacomo Agostini (MV Agusta, left) and runner-up Phil Read (Yamaha, right) link hands with Honda-mounted winner Jim Redman: Junior TT, 1965.

Opposite: Friends at last! Or perhaps not. Jorge Lorenzo and impertinent 2013 rival Marc Marquez look unconvinced at a formal making-up session. They'd clashed fairings in Jerez, and angry Lorenzo got the worst of it.

1952

Facing the Press

MUCH HAS CHANGED IN 60 YEARS of Grand Prix racing. One thing is the role of the Press. In gentler times, top riders and the relatively small number of regular GP reporters shared time and friendship before and after the races. In some cases, very close friendships.

They also shared secrets. Post-race parties were often wild affairs, and in the 1960s especially cocaine and pills were in a small number of cases an imperfectly concealed secret. The reporters of the time knew about it, but wouldn't dream of writing about it.

How different now. At each race more than 200 journalists and broadcasters crowd the Press room, each seeking a scoop of his own. And as top international sportsmen, the senior riders are cocooned in protective layers of PR men and publicity agents. Journalists' time with them is severely rationed and controlled. Clever riders practise sound-bites for the cameras and conferences (Rossi is a past master), while others shrink from the limelight. Uniform-clad sponsorship types hang around to see that nothing controversial is said.

And if there was even a whiff of a scandal, it would be all over the internet within minutes. Luckily, riders are still prepared to spill a little passion from time to time. As when race-winner Rossi and then deadly rival Max Biaggi had a physical spat on the way to the Catalunya rostrum of 2001, leaving Biaggi with a spot of blood on his cheek. Asked at the subsequent Press conference what had happened, he glared at Rossi, then replied: "A mosquito bit me."

Left: An older rider faces some gentle post-race probing in 1952 from a smart radio interviewer.

Right: Mobbed by the Press! It's not only the fans who fight to get close to Valentino Rossi.

Left: Eight years old and with racing in his blood, future double champion Barry Sheene helps fettle his father Frank's Itom-based "Sheene Special" in 1958.

Opposite: Marc Marquez first raced aged five, was road-racing at eight, and before he was 21 had become youngest-ever World Champion. Beat that.

1958

Early Starters

RECORDS ARE FRAGILE IN RACING – but two will stand for the foreseeable future.

The youngest rider ever to start in a GP was Jorge Lorenzo. The 2010 MotoGP champion missed the first day of practice for the 2002 Spanish GP at Jerez, but turned 15 the next day and was eligible to ride. He qualified 33rd and finished 22nd.

The youngest-ever GP winner is Briton Scott Redding – his home 125 GP at 15 years and 170 days. Since then, the minimum age has been raised again: back to 16.

Other "youngest-ever" records remain in jeopardy, with today's generation of riders having started racing before turning seven and turned full-time as teenagers.

This being so, the achievement of British youngsters Mike Hailwood and John Surtees is impressive. Hailwood is still the fourth-youngest premier-class champion, at 22 years and 160 days (1962, MV Agusta). Surtees was only 15 days older (1956, MV Agusta). Most of their rivals were in their 30s.

Youngest top-class champion is new-century star Marc Marquez: 20 years and 266 days old in 2013. In 1983, Freddie Spencer was 21 and 258 days; Casey Stoner (2007) was 84 days older. Marquez also became the youngest premier-class race winner at the GP of the Americas in 2013, 63 days past his 20th birthday.

The tide of youth is inexorable. This makes Loris Capirossi's record more impressive. In 1990 he became the youngest champion in the 125 class, aged 17 years and 165 days. It was his first season. The only other 17-year-old champion is Marc Marquez in 2010, almost 100 days older and in his third season. To cap it, Capirossi was in 2011 the oldest rider on the MotoGP grid.

1962

Racing Wives

THE MOST FAMOUS RACING WIFE in Grand Prix history is without a doubt Stephanie Sheene. That's because when the slinky blonde glamour model turned up at the Austrian GP in 1976 on the arm of reigning champion Barry Sheene, she was actually somebody else's wife ... and the British newspapers had a front-page field day. Stephanie and Barry did eventually get married, after he'd retired from racing and after they'd had a son and a daughter. All the while she'd been a role model for that difficult part – sitting and waiting in the pit box while your man goes out and risks his neck. Again.

Another famous champion, 1970s/80s German star Anton Mang's wife Collette was even closer to the racing effort. Collette was Anton's manager, agent, interpreter as well as constant companion. She filled the anxious hours with stopwatches and lap charts: her data was used at least once to settle time-keeping disputes. Nowadays electronics fills that role, while a top rider even has a man ready to hand him his gloves and polish his visor for him when he arrives in the pits.

At the same time, increasing numbers of pit personnel and higher levels of professionalism have seen wives (and other family members) banned from the pits on several instances.

Which makes Casey Stoner's willowy young wife somewhat exceptional. They wed when he was just 21 and yet to win the 2006 title, and Adriana is ever-present by his side as his grid girl, waiting patiently and decoratively in the pit; also sitting quietly in the third or fourth row at the post-race Press conference.

Above: Not the normal honeymoon – racing wives handled the fiddly jobs in the old days, like applying racing numbers.

Opposite: Casey Stoner's young Australian wife Adriana was his constant companion and grid girl. This is at Motegi, in his championship year of 2007.

1955

Family Connections

WHAT KIND OF FATHER sends his son out motorbike racing? Often, it's one who indulged in the sport in his own young days – but in the case of the first and so far only father-and-son World Championship combination, Kenny Roberts insists that he tried everything to stop his son Kenny Junior from becoming a professional racer: "He needed to really want to do it, in spite of me." Kenny, spearheading an American invasion, was 500cc World Champion from 1978–80: "Junior" repeated the feat in 2000.

Father-and-son success began when the son of the first-ever World Champion, Les Graham, won the first of two GPs at the Isle of Man in 1967. That was Stuart Graham, who moved on early to a car racing career. Two years later, Alberto Pagani won the first of his three races: his father Nello had claimed four wins in 1949 and Alberto was first to achieve the feat in the 500 class.

More famously, Valentino Rossi's dad Graziano had been a GP winner in his time, though his tally of three, in the 250 class, doesn't compare with his son's 105 and still counting. Spanish small-class specialist "Aspar" Martinez raced against both and when beaten by the son, whom he had met as a babe-in-arms in the paddock, quipped: "I should have run him over when I had the chance."

Pablo Nieto, son of the legendary Angel, claimed one win to his father's 90; most recently German Stefan Bradl took five Moto2 wins and the 2011 title: dad Helmut claimed five 250 wins in 1991. Clearly, in some cases, racing is in the genes.

Left: Jack and John – the Surtees family. The burly bike shop owner and amateur racer shepherded his son to the top – here at the 1955 West German GP at the Nürburgring.

Right: The first father-and-son 500cc champions. Kenny Roberts Junior won the premier championship in 2000 and father "King" Kenny had done so from 1978 to 1980.

1964

The Trappings of Success

LIKE POP MUSIC, the very big money in bike racing is reserved for a few top acts.

This has always been so. What has changed is the scale. A top racer before the 1970s could amass a tidy sum: Mike Hailwood was well able to indulge his taste for Iso-Grifo sports cars, while investing in property and business at home and abroad. But from the mid-1980s onwards, as sponsorship and TV kicked in, the amounts multiplied into many millions.

Status symbols often had four wheels. John Surtees was pleased to be given a BMW 507 coupe by Count Agusta in 1956 and the rare car remains in his garage to this day.

Barry Sheene was of a flashier period and had a series of Rolls-Royces with the number-plate BSR 4. Friend and self-styled slipstreamer Steve Parrish followed suit: his Rolls was famously numbered PEN 1 S.

Then came the motorhomes: Mamola's had a built-in golf cart; Kevin Schwantz's had a Suzuki jeep in a trailer slung behind.

Watery adventure beckoned a newer generation: Mick Doohan went boating on a bigger and bigger scale, terrifying his companions as he tackled giant ocean swells at full speed. He followed Sheene and Daryl Beattie into helicopters, and now includes an executive air fleet business as part of a diverse business empire.

The biggest earner of all time is Rossi, whose 2012 earnings estimated at US $30 million put him 20th on the Forbes list of highest-paid athletes. He took a salary cut in 2013/14 moving back to Yamaha from Ducati, but the success of his VR46 brand combined with a growing property portfolio plus a $1.2-million Pershing 56 motor yacht helped preserve his name on the rich list.

Right: Family fortunes – Britain's multiple champion John Surtees followed his father into the motorcycle business.

Opposite: Modern racing success can bring great reward. Here, Mr and Mrs Loris Capirossi lounge on a yacht in Italy in 2009.

1950

Autograph Hunters

THEY COME IN HORDES, shuffling feet, screaming and jostling. Nobody's quite sure how they got in, but it means Valentino's around.

That was in the earlier days of his popularity. By 2011, some teams employed armed guards in case too many people managed to slip past the ever-tighter security.

To some riders, signing autographs can be an irritation or even a grim duty, undertaken at a sponsor's behest. But to Barry Sheene, first of the self-made superstars, it was a duty to make it look like a pleasure. His wife Stephanie recalled how they would stay for hours after a big event, with a line of fans through the paddock. Barry always told her: the traffic will be jammed up anyway. Might as well do this. And so he did: with a cheery smile and a cheeky remark for people who would cherish the encounter for ever.

Access to the stars was easier in the early days. Race paddocks were informally enclosed, if at all; riders camped alongside their motorcycles and the fans could wander around as much as they dared.

Today it's rationed and organized. To get a big star's genuine autograph – rather than a signed poster handed out by a PR girl – is quite an achievement.

The autographs are worth everything to the true collector, with very little on the open market – there's no trade in the scrawls. But they verify a personal contact and for many, that's enough to make them priceless.

Left: Autograph hunters tackle a competitor before the Isle of Man Senior Tourist Trophy (TT) in the 1950s.

Right: Valentino Rossi signs hats, notebooks and posters at Mugello in 2005.

1967

The Victory Celebration

WHEN WINNING IS EVERYTHING, the accomplishment can be overwhelming. Seldom more so than for Jorge Lorenzo, who had to be helped to safety after being in danger of drowning. He'd just won his home GP at Jerez in 2010, but his leap into the lake in front of the final grandstands was as ill-judged as it was exuberant.

Mike Hailwood would restrict himself to a cheeky wave to a friend (often even before the race had finished). He and his pal Bill Ivy once dressed up as flower-children, Mike in a long blond wig, but that was before the races had been won.

Celebratory wheelies and tyre-frazzling burn-outs marked the early years of the over-powered 500s, while riders would often slow to be handed a national flag by pre-primed supporters.

But it was Rossi who ushered in a new theatrical era. It started as simple costume drama in his 250 years (Robin Hood for the British GP, Gothic knight with studded mace at the Nürburging, beach boy in Italy), then moved on to pantomime with a series of tableaux – a speeding ticket at the Italian GP, in a ball-and-chain at Brno, running to the toilet at Jerez (his own favourite) and seven dwarves after his seventh World Championship.

Lorenzo then added to his own amateur dramatics with his trademark "Lorenzo's Land" flag planted in the gravel at each new country where he won, plus a variety of other performances from rock star to moonwalker.

It's contrived, it's TV-friendly and in the mood after a good race, it's always fun.

Left: Another day, another wreath.
Giacomo Agostini takes the spoils at
Mallory Park's post-TT meeting in 1967.

Right: Spain's Jorge Lorenzo
executes a perfectly controlled
"Flying W" after winning at Brno in 2010.

1967

Two-man Show

HOW MANY TO MAKE A RACE? Some of the finest years have been played out between just two. Great rivals make great racing; for the riders as well. As Wayne Rainey and Kevin Schwantz agree: "We each elevated the other."

The pair's battles remain legend, all the way from the USA to the World Championship: close and spectacular. Rainey won three titles to Schwantz's one but the lanky Texan had 25 wins to Rainey's 24.

Racing duets echo through history. Freddie Spencer and Eddie Lawson in the 1980s swapped the title to and fro, but their races were seldom close. Spencer and Kenny Roberts, however, raged by inches all year long until the last race of 1983. Only then did Fast Freddie depose King Kenny, winning Honda's first top-class title.

The 1960s were richest for hand-to-hand fighting. For two years Mike Hailwood's Honda versus Giacomo Agostini's MV Agusta played an eight-cylinder two-hander. Hailwood failed to win Honda's first 500 title by the narrowest margin. They finished 1967 equal on 46 points and five wins apiece, but Ago took the honours: he had three second places, Hailwood only two.

Hailwood and Phil Read made a two-man show in the smaller classes; likewise Read and Jim Redman, and Read and Bill Ivy. The difference in the last case was that they were team-mates and rebel Phil broke Yamaha's orders in winning both 125 and 250 titles in 1968.

Right: Ago and Hailwood, Hailwood and Ago – the two great champions spent most of 1967 inches apart. Giacomo Agostini (1) rode the MV Agusta, Mike Hailwood the Honda. Ago won in the end.

Opposite: The all-American duel of Wayne Rainey (3) and Kevin Schwantz (34) spilled on to the world stage for five memorable years between 1989 and 1993. Here they battle at Britain's Donington Park in 1969.

1953

On the Podium

VICTORY IS SWEET ... and once used to be dignified. Sporting celebrations have been revolutionized over six decades of bike Grand Prix racing, however. The restrained and chaste kiss from a girl in national costume and the handshake with the Mayor have given way to champagne-sprays so violent that the dignitaries are forced to stand well clear.

In less formal times, riders would be surrounded by fans sharing the moment. Nowadays it is more exclusive: the top three are partitioned off in *parc fermé* and get their hugs over a barrier before being ushered to a remote rostrum by security guards.

Champagne-spraying is also a more modern phenomenon and a useful release from the high tension of the race for the riders, who would prefer to be celebrating with their friends, family and teams. It's also another chance for winning riders to put one in the eye of those they have beaten ... sometimes literally. John Kocinski was not the last rider who had to be led off the rostrum partially blinded after he finished second to Mick Doohan at Jerez in 1991.

Right: New 125 World Champion Werner Haas gets understated congratulations after winning the Grand Prix of Nations at Monza on his NSU in 1953.

Opposite: Surrounded by so great a cloud of witnesses: Marquez and Honda dominated the 2014 return to Argentina, with team-mate Dani Pedrosa second, Jorge Lorenzo (Yamaha) third, and the fans in ecstasy.

1953

The Team Together

IN MODERN RACING, a team travels the world for more than half the year, always in one another's company and generally in uniform. The military connotations are unavoidable and the groups can be as tight-knit as a crack army platoon.

The same spirit was present back in the days when team managers wore ties and mechanics sported scruffy overalls – although in days of yore, the rider himself would have his hand on the spanners too, as often as not. In the best cases, a pit crew will team up with a particular rider, and stay with him. Like Nobby Clark with Mike Hailwood or Kel Carruthers with Kenny Roberts.

For more than a two-man partnership, there is no better example than Barry Sheene, who went all the way from club racing to the 500 World Championship with his father Frank and long-term mechanic Don Mackay. They were finally, forcibly, replaced by factory professionals only after an oversight in brake assembly cost Barry a race.

The finest example, however, comes from the modern era and stayed together until 2013: it is the predominantly antipodean pit crew led by Jerry Burgess, with fellow-Australian Alex Briggs as his right-hand man. In a reign that so far includes 13 World Championship wins (one with Wayne Gardner, five with Mick Doohan and seven with Valentino Rossi) other Australians have come and gone from the squad, but Kiwi Brent Stephens has been a constant, as has Belgian Bernhard Ansiau and Briton Gary Coleman.

In a surprise move, however, Rossi replaced Burgess with a fellow-Italian for 2014. Burgess's long reign was over.

Left: The German factory NSU team crowd round 125 winner Werner Haas at the Dutch TT of 1953 – his first win of the championship year.

Right: The 2010 Fiat Yamaha team frame riders Jorge Lorenzo and Valentino Rossi at a pre-season unveiling at Sepang, Malaysia.

1952

Champagne Moments

WHEN DID IT BEGIN, the oh-so-macho ritual of spraying champagne from the rostrum? Nobody in racing now seems quite sure, but photographs prove that when the world was in black-and-white race winners were content to stand politely at attention and laurel-wreathed for the anthems.

After a race the atmosphere is unique. The smell of victory combines adrenalin-sweat on leather with baking tyres and even hotter metal.

Riders stand tall on graded steps, winner in the middle, hear the winner's national anthem (usually, though at Laguna Seca in 2010 they mistakenly greeted Spanish winner Jorge Lorenzo with the jaunty Italian tune of third-place Valentino Rossi), and then comes the bubbly.

In the modern era, Spanish cava has replaced French champagne, reflecting the 1993 take-over by Dorna. But nowadays, it's not for everybody.

The opening of GP racing to younger riders (15 in the late 1990s and early 2000s but now raised to 16) led to a new phenomenon: 125 race winners too young to be allowed champagne on the rostrum. Lemonade must suffice.

Left: British champions Geoff Duke (left) and car racer Stirling Moss share a cuppa at Goodwood in the 1950s.

Opposite: Putting some fizz into winning: Jorge Lorenzo (front), Dani Pedrosa (left) and Casey Stoner splash it all about in Catalunya in 2010.

Right: Multiple champion Mike
Hailwood basks in the reflection
of his trophy collection.

Opposite: Casey Stoner won his
home GP in Australia in 2009 –
and took home a carbon-fibre hub-cap.

Trophy Moments

HOW SWEET THE MOMENT when you hold the trophy aloft. Or, in Mike Hailwood's case, dangle a huge collection of them from a length of string.

Prizes for racers have changed.

For many years, it was the money that counted. Low-placed finishers would hope for enough to pay for petrol to the next race; the winners would celebrate with champagne. That changed for good in the 1980s, after rider strikes and teams' association IRTA won a better financial package for all.

Nowadays the (much) bigger money for the winners comes from team and sponsor bonuses.

One thing has stayed constant – the trophy presented to the winner is always bigger than those for second and third.

Fashions, ever mercurial, have changed from the classic silver cups and wing-footed statuettes. Today's winners are more likely to be handed some modern art in crystal. No matter: they all adorn the trophy cupboard.

One of the better trophies came not from officials but from a fan. Max Biaggi had won the 250 race at Jerez in 1996 in fine style and halfway through the lap of honour was handed a whole Spanish jamon. His swerving ride back to the pits, this fine large joint of ham swinging from his wrist, struck a chord with anyone who has ridden a motorcycle or even a bicycle with a shopping bag dangling from one handlebar.

1951

Meeting the Public

WHEN JORGE LORENZO WON the MotoGP World Championship in 2010, his reception in his home town on the island of Mallorca was like a national feast day. Crowds lined the road from the airport to the presidential palace in Palma de Mallorca and massed in the square as he waved from the balcony alongside the President.

As far as meeting the public goes, it was an extreme example. For the rest of his week off, Lorenzo withdrew to quiet solitude with his family.

It's the same for all of today's big stars, their fame pumped by TV and national fervour. "Meeting the people" often comprises waving at them from behind a barrier patrolled by security guards. Such is the life of a modern sporting superstar. Rossi once told me, when asked if there was anything he would like to change: "My face – to see what it is like not to be Valentino Rossi."

To meet a racing star face to face is every fan's dream. Such encounters were always possible in the old days: one simply had to hang around the paddock. With patience and persistence you might bump into Geoff Duke or Umberto Masetti. Now the pleasure is reserved mainly for sponsors' guests and racing insiders.

Popular figures such as Geoff Duke, Mike Hailwood, Giacomo Agostini and especially Barry Sheene understood the value of the public. Some of today's stars however shrink from the limelight – Casey Stoner and Daniel Pedrosa being in sharp contrast to Rossi and Lorenzo.

Left: Within touching distance. Cheering crowds brave the rain as 1951 Ulster GP winner Geoff Duke (Norton) strides towards the rostrum.

Opposite: Adoring fans in their thousands invade Germany's Sachsenring pit lane for a glimpse of 2009 winner Rossi. Just count the yellow hats.

Above: Helped by his father Jack (left) and a mechanic, battered John Surtees hobbles painfully away from a crash at Assen in 1960.

Opposite: Dani Pedrosa thumps into the Airfence in Germany in 2008. He escaped with ankle injuries, a broken finger, and a ruined title campaign.

1960

Bumps

HITTING THE BARRIERS has a whole different meaning in modern racing. The speeds may have been lower in the early days, but not enough to make much difference when the trackside furniture was a hard straw bale, a stone bank or even a tree.

Trackside protection has been revolutionized, step by step. It has often been an agonizing process. Disastrous experiments with catch-fencing in the 1970s resulted in fatalities – designed for cars, their poles were weakened at the base to absorb energy as they snapped. But a motorcyclist's body wasn't heavy enough: unprotected Armco barrier also took a deadly toll.

Gradually the needs of cars and bikes were reconciled; barriers were moved back, gravel run-offs installed or extended, hopefully preventing impact but at least slowing it down.

Lately a new fashion has arisen for paved run-off areas, but some riders (Casey Stoner in the lead) excoriate them for they give a rider a second chance if he overshoots the corner. "If you make a mistake, you should be punished," says the Australian.

Without question the greatest contribution to motorcycle racing safety was the Airfence, developed in Australia and introduced from the mid-1990s. It has proved its worth at absorbing impact time and again, and is now standard trackside furniture at danger spots.

Several riders owe their lives to this scientifically applied bouncy castle, most notably Daniel Pedrosa's Svengali Alberto Puig, after an ultra-high-speed crash at Le Mans in 1995.

1982

Back in the Saddle

THE GREATEST COMEBACK FALLS to the heroic figure of Mike Hailwood. Nine times World Champion, he had quit in 1968 and spent the next decade F1 racing and dallying with various far-flung business enterprises. Then in 1978 he decided to return to contest the Isle of Man TT.

Everyone expected the emotion: Mike had won the island race 12 times at the height of his career when it was still a World Championship round. Nobody expected that now; they'd reckoned without Mike the Bike. After 11 years away, he won the Formula One TT and came back the next year to win the Senior TT as well.

Modern medical techniques combine with rider determination have seen some remarkable feats. In 2013 Jorge Lorenzo broke his collarbone on the first day of practice for the Dutch TT. The bone was screwed together that night, and he returned to race to a brave if tearful fifth place.

A haunting example was in 1992. Mick Doohan was running away with the title when he broke his leg in Holland. Questionable medical care caused massive complications – he spent three weeks with his legs sewn together. After two months, looking like a ghost, he came back for the last two races. He was too weak to stop Wayne Rainey powering past to win by four points.

In 2010, Rossi set a new speed record: back in action 41 days after suffering a compound fracture to his leg ... only to be eclipsed later the same year by Randy de Puniet, who sustained a similar injury and was racing again after 26 days.

Left: Father Frank and mechanic Ken Fletcher (left) help Barry Sheene into the saddle of his Yamaha – his first time on a bike since smashing both legs in 1982.

Right: Kazuto Sakata was 125cc champion in 1994 and 1998. Here in 1996 he rests his injured leg in the bike garage.

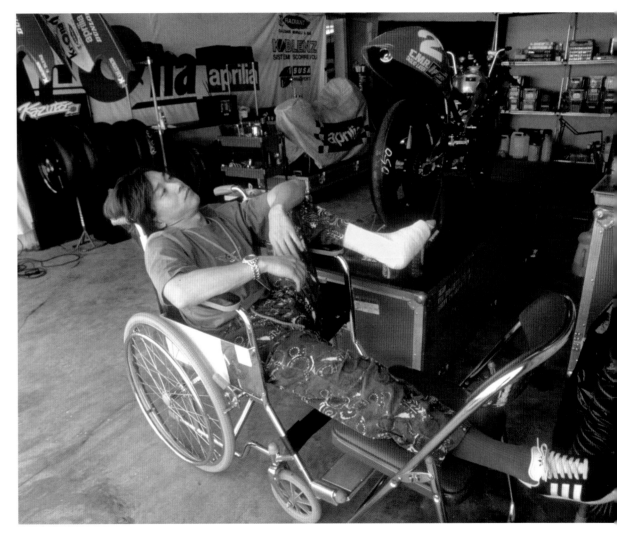

1993

Crashes

CRASHES ARE COMMONPLACE IN RACING. Bad crashes increasingly rare. Better rider safety equipment and much safer circuits are the reason why.

And it is bad crashes that forced the pace of this development – generally thanks to action from the riders after the event.

One such signal event happened in 1977 at the Salzburgring, in the 350cc race. World Champion Franco Uncini set it underway with a simple slide-away crash in one of the steep-sided mountainside circuit's very fast corners. But instead of sliding safely into a gravel trap, the narrow confines meant that his bike bounced back and skittled close rivals in the front group. Fellow champions Dieter Braun and Johnny Ceccotto were among those badly injured in a scene of destruction strewn with straw bales, crashed motorbikes and bewildered officials. But it was lesser-known rider Hans Stadelmann who died when he ploughed into the wreckage with no warning from overwhelmed marshals.

The 500-class riders, led by Barry Sheene, staged a strike and as a result, marshalling standards were immediately improved, while the safety features (or their absence) became more of a talking point.

Multiple crashes like this are most feared by the riders: collisions with solid objects (like other motorbikes) cause the worst injuries. They are still a feature of racing in the crowded Moto2 class, where 40 starters on almost identical motorbikes frequently have trouble all getting round the first corner.

Left: Not a classic Grand Prix, but it hurts just the same. Britain's late TT star David Jefferies loops over a fallen machine at the 1993 Macao GP.

Opposite: It's landing that hurts. Aleix Espargaro is in the air, Alvaro Bautista (19) about to join him. Randy de Puniet (right) was the first to fall, and the only injury victim, with a broken leg.

1954

Last Respects

FOUR YEARS AFTER BECOMING the first 500-class World Champion, Les Graham crashed fatally during the Isle of Man TT. Amazingly, given the number of fatalities in the first two decades of GP racing, the Briton remains the only premier-class champion to have paid the ultimate price while racing a motorcycle.

The list of last respects is long and heavily biased towards the early years. Every loss is tragic, but some were important for other reasons.

The fatal accidents to Spanish 250 star Santiago Herrero in 1970 and 125 title-leading Italian Gilberto Parlotti in 1972, both at the Isle of Man TT, cast long shadows. Spanish racers were forbidden to return, while the Italian MV Agusta team also pulled out. Other top riders also refused to be compelled to race on the long, fast and desperately dangerous TT circuit, and after 1976 it was dropped from the Championship calendar.

Another double-fatality postponed a racing milestone. Finnish 250 champion Jarno Saarinen was heading the 500 class in 1973 riding a two-stroke Yamaha when he died, along with Italian Renzo Pasolini, in a ghastly first-lap multiple pile-up at Monza. Yamaha withdrew for the rest of the season.

Fatalities are mercifully rare in modern times. The last rider to pay with his life was former 250 champion and rising MotoGP star Marco Simoncelli, in Malaysia in 2011; one year after inaugural Moto2 race winner Shoya Tomizawa. They were the first since Daijiro Kato died at his home Japanese GP seven years before.

May they all rest in peace.

Right: German GP racers Hermann Paul Müller, Werner Haas and Hans Baltisberger and Austrian Rupert Hollaus pay tribute at the Jimmy Guthrie memorial on the Isle of Man. Pre-war hero Guthrie died at the German GP.

Opposite: Riders, officials, racing staff and fans pay respect to Marco Simoncelli at Valencia in 2011, killed at the previous round. His family requested "a minute of noise": his white Honda led a crescendo of exhausts.

1964

Racing Cars and Bikes

BIKE RACERS THINK CAR RACING must be easy – sitting and twiddling a wheel, the car doing the work. In a few notable cases they have been proved right. The skills are different, but can overlap.

Many is the bike World Champion who has proved little better than average in a car. Geoff Duke was fast enough in a brief stint in Aston Martin sports cars, but felt badly treated and did not continue; Eddie Lawson fell short of greatness on four wheels. Conversely, mid-field GP racer Steve Parrish later became four-times European (effectively World) Champion ... in truck racing.

Only John Surtees has won both senior championships. He was four times 500cc champion between 1956 and 1960. Then in 1964 he won the F1 Championship in a Ferrari. He later became a team owner with a car bearing his name ... driven by Mike Hailwood.

Hailwood distinguished himself, never winning a GP but earning the George Medal in 2006 for his heroic rescue of Clay Regazzoni from his burning car.

His bike contemporary Bill Ivy made a stunning car debut in top-level F2 in Britain and was lauded for his huge natural talent, but died in a bike crash only weeks later. In contrast, 1961 double champion Gary Hocking quit bikes in 1962 because of the danger, but died in an F1 car later that year in South Africa.

Can Valentino Rossi follow Surtees? Flirtation with Ferrari meant several tests ... but Rossi found the atmosphere not to his liking. He remained committed to his first love: motorcycles.

Left: Will he or won't he? Rossi has tested a Ferrari F1 car several times – here in 2006. But bike racing is his greater love.

Opposite: The only World Champion on two and four wheels, John Surtees in his title-winning Ferrari in 1964.

High Jinks

RACERS' HIGH JINKS CAN EASILY GET OUT OF CONTROL. They often involve crazy antics in rented cars, with several very narrow escapes and to be honest, at least one fatal crash. Some include high explosives.

One such incident famously involved Barry Sheene. Disgusted by the paddock lavatories in 1971 in Finland, he threw firecrackers down the pit. The subsequent explosion burned down the wooden buildings.

Almost 20 years later, Randy Mamola developed a taste for increasingly large and powerful firecrackers; disrupting paddock and pits at all hours until eventually authorities put a stop to it.

Mamola, once styled Clown Prince of racing, loved practical jokes but needed some help from Kevin Schwantz and Eddie Lawson in the great Porsche débâcle of 1989. Porsche lent each one of the brand-new 944 S2 models as a promotion to drive between the German GP at Hockenheim and the Austrian GP at Salzburgring a week later. Travelling in convoy they called on Venice on the way, where the first collision came when Schwantz stopped suddenly, Lawson close behind. Mamola cannoned into both of them from behind. They got the cars, now quite a bit shorter, to Austria, only for Lawson to put his almost upside down in a ditch.

The vehicles were a sorry sight when Porsche took them back. Schwantz recalled: "They said: as long as no one else was involved, no problem."

No such understanding from Max Biaggi, when he awoke in the Mugello paddock to find his new Smart car overturned by rivals. They didn't like the self-promoting paint scheme ... or the rider.

Left: World Champion Barry Sheene and his then girlfriend Stephanie McLean could do push-bike acrobatics too.

Opposite: How d'you get a helmet over that? Valentino Rossi is flanked by Sete Gibernau (left) and Loris Capirossi after winning at Valencia in 2003.

Two

The Machines

Right: The search for speed led to some spaceship bodywork, until "dustbin fairings" were banned on safety grounds. This is the NSU Sportmax 250 in 1955.

Above: Innovation in action – 1966 champion Luigi Taveri Honda's RC149 had a unique in-line five-cylinder engine of just 125cc.

Opposite: Same number of cylinders, different era. The Honda RC211V V5 was the most successful new-generation 990cc MotoGP machine. This is Nicky Hayden.

1966

Great Inventions

WHAT SUCCEEDS IN RACING, according to former champion and great engineer Kel Carruthers, is: "what worked last year ... plus a few per cent." Innovation is risk.

To put it another way: copy, but improve. Racing's role in engineering lies in development rather than invention: engines, tyres, suspension and components have all been tried and tested on the track. The journey to the road is short because road and race bikes are close relations.

This makes the handful of genuine inventions stand out all the more. Particularly that of German MZ engineer Walter Kaaden, who crystallized his experience with the pulse-jet V1 bombs of the 1939–45 World War into an understanding of the two-stroke engine's acoustic pulsing. Using disc valves and resonant exhaust chambers on a shoe-string budget, he invented the high-performance two-stroke in the late 1950s: a breed that would come to dominate racing until outlawed in favour of big four-strokes, 50 years later.

Most other innovations have been borrowed from elsewhere. Even Ducati's exclusive desmodromic (positive-closing) valve gear wasn't new even when they pioneered its racing use in the late 1950s. The Italians have developed the principle to an art form ever since.

Honda perfected high-revving multi-cylinder engines in racing, then in the late 1960s the four-cylinder K750 put a GP race replica on every street. Yamaha and Suzuki turned Kaaden's ideas into a generation of fine sports bikes.

For the rest, look to detail, such as the twin-beam chassis credited to Spanish engineer Antonio Cobas, and Yamaha's new-century cross-plane crankshaft. And into the most inventive area of all – electronics.

Above: Bullet nose helped Bill Lomas to win the 1955 Junior TT, but instability in crosswinds meant this effective streamlining development was banned.

Opposite: Radically wrong – Honda's 1979 four-stroke NR500 used oval pistons and a monocoque chassis to challenged the two-strokes. It did not score a single point.

1955

Failures

THERE ARE WAYS OF MEASURING FAILURE, but in racing it's quite simple. Results mean everything. Giving rise to a string of failures, often very noble failures, but failures all the same.

It started at the beginning. When the World Championship was born in 1949, one significant change from the old pre-war European Championship was that supercharging was banned. This at a stroke turned two exciting machines into scrap metal: the AJS V4

... Les Graham won the inaugural title on a simpler twin-cylinder 500 and the Velocette "Roarer", a longitudinal twin. Both had been designed around integral supercharging.

Other failures came about through an excess of engineering ambition. The V8 Moto-Guzzi was a wonderful and sonorous machine but cannot be counted as a success since it so seldom ran effectively on all eight cylinders. A more modern example came from noted F1 engine firm Ilmor. Their 800 built for 2007 used high-revving F1 engine techniques: the result was powerful, but impossible to ride fast – motorcycles need a more rider-friendly engine – and the Ilmor pulled out after only a couple of races.

Most magnificent of all follies was built by Honda. With radical oval pistons and eight-valve cylinder heads, the four-stroke engine of the NR500 was meant to challenge the reigning 500 two-strokes and it was clad in an equally radical "clam-shell" monocoque chassis, with pioneering "inverted" forks. It was disastrously unsuccessful, struggling even to qualify, and never scoring a single point.

Honda had to build a hated two-stroke to achieve premier-class success.

1975

Two-stroke to Four-stroke

JULY 27, 1958 WAS AN IMPORTANT DATE in racing. It was then at Hedemora in Sweden that East German rider Horst Fügner claimed the first-ever Grand Prix victory for a two-stroke motorcycle. He was riding a 250 MZ and defeated Mike Hailwood's four-stroke NSU by one-and-a-half minutes. Fügner went on to finish second in the world.

It was the beginning of the end for four-strokes in Grand Prix racing, though it was not until 1974 that a two-stroke Yamaha finally deposed the mighty MV Agusta from the premier class title. It had come by stages: Suzuki's first 50cc title in 1962 followed by 125cc and 250cc in the ensuing years.

Two-strokes were removed from the opposite end: concern from the industry that the 500cc two-strokes were too far removed from their top-selling 1000cc four-stroke sports bikes meant the death sentence at the end of 2001, when the top class was opened to 990cc four-strokes.

Riders like Valentino Rossi came to love the 990s, but at the time he led the chorus of regret that the lightweight two-strokes had gone.

Like it or not, the breed was doomed. Next to go was the 250cc class, which had withered on the vine by the time the replacement 600cc four-stroke Moto2 class was launched one year earlier than planned in 2010.

By the end of 2011 the 125s would also run out of time: replaced by Moto3 – 250cc single-cylinder four-strokes.

Their passing was mourned but in the big classes time had shown they would not be missed for long.

Left: The OW23 was Yamaha's first 500cc racer. Multiple four-stroke champion Giacomo Agostini rode it to the first two-stroke title in 1975.

Right: Honda confrontation. Alex Barros's two-stroke 500 leads Valentino Rossi's 990cc four-stroke at Assen in 2002. The contest was close, but the four-stroke won.

1954

Side View

THE SILHOUETTE OF A GRAND PRIX MOTORCYCLE is determined by two main factors: fashion and regulations. Rules dictate that all of the front wheel and half of the rear must be visible. The size of the mudguards is dictated; also the width of bodywork and the length of both nose and tailpiece.

The fashion is both technical – especially near-identical suspension front and rear – and driven by the marketing department. Sports-bike styling cross-fertilizes MotoGP, and vice versa. Scoops and paint-jobs apart, the basic pattern is pretty similar.

It was not always so. Early dustbin fairings concealed not only the wheels but almost everything else as well, including a far greater variety of suspension ideas and engine configurations than today.

Dustbins took the blame for instability and even crashes in windy conditions, although the better designs were able to compensate, but they were blanket-banned anyway in 1957, and the so-called "dolphin" fairing has been enforced ever since to the continuing dismay of all aerodynamic boffins.

The scant bodywork does have one advantage for spectators: they can see the whole of the rider and exactly what he is doing. Maybe that's better than streamlining.

Right: Long, with a low-slung horizontal cylinder, the 1954 Moto Guzzi had an elegant simplicity.

Opposite: The last-ever 250cc champion Hiro Aoyama uses tyre smoke to accent the elegant lines of his Honda 250 in 2009.

1955

Head-on

THE FRONTAL ASPECT OF A RACING MOTORCYCLE projects its purpose. It always has, of course, but it has changed radically.

Back in the first years, when bikes were naked, they all looked much the same from in front. Variety came through the 1950s with painted dustbin fairings but the regulation dolphin since then made them all look similar once more.

Yet there is surprising variety in that simple design: from Honda's compact and jagged manga-like approach, accentuated by colour-contrast graphics, to the smooth curves of the all-red Ducati. Nor would one confuse a Yamaha with a Suzuki.

The first goal is a small frontal area, with a fairing that cuts the air cleanest when the rider is tucked in behind. The second is to flow the air to engine and radiators, and out again. After that, the third can be applied: brand identification. For Moto Guzzi in the 1950s it was simply trade-mark green anodizing for the all-enveloping aluminium cowl (paint would only add weight). Every make has its signature.

Identification goes beyond the marque. Regulations stipulate that the racing number must be clearly visible from the front. Until the early 1990s these were colour-coded: black on yellow for 500s; white on green for 350s, on blue for 250s and on black for 125s. But by now sponsors were clamouring to integrate their own colours and liveries.

Jazzier and increasingly illegible designs proliferated. And by 2011 a new rule demanded easy-to-read numbers once more.

Right: This Moto Guzzi, with Bill Lomas aboard, shows how the designer went for maximum penetration with a very low profile.

Opposite: Rules now dictate that front wheels must be fully visible. The rest of the Ducati's curves, here ridden by Nicky Hayden and Mika Kallio, are shaped in the wind-tunnel.

1953

Engines

WHAT A VARIETY OF ENGINES over the years. From one cylinder to eight, with every possible variation in between. Vee configurations have come in from two cylinders to five (no GP V6 as yet). There have been two-strokes and four-strokes; air-cooled and water-cooled. And they still haven't all agreed yet on the perfect design.

As ever the early years saw more variety and experiment. Moto Guzzi's V8 of 1955 was a highlight. But like the fascinating and innovative Honda NR500, with eight valves, oval pistons and a rev ceiling of more than 20,000 rpm, it was a failure.

Moto Guzzi was ever innovative: as well as several fine singles, their 500 V-twin had the cylinders splayed out wide at 120 degrees ... it was very long and very low.

After the Italian factory withdrawal in 1957, renegade MV Agusta led a sterile period of domination with a sonorous twin-cam four-cylinder: an engine style pioneered by Italian rivals Rondine and later, Gilera.

The two-strokes killed MV in 1974. It took another 20 years before convention dictated V4 500s; then in the new century they were in turn killed off by new rules opening the former 500 class to 990cc four-strokes.

Cue another rich period. Honda's V5 RC211V was dominant, but by the time the 800s arrived in 2007 everyone had settled on some kind of V4 ... whether real, like those of Ducati, Honda and Suzuki, or virtual, such as Yamaha's cleverly re-engineered cross-plane crankshaft in-line M1 engine.

In 2012, the engines went back to 1000cc, but now four cylinders with a maximum bore size were enshrined in increasingly strict regulations.

Left: Designed by Piero Remor, son of Rondine and Gilera, the four-cylinder MV 500 was a thing of beauty, proudly displayed by rider Hermann Paul Müller in 1953.

Opposite: A modern bike hides its engine. Crash damage reveals only a little more of Valentino Rossi's M1 Yamaha, at Mugello in 2010. Rossi broke his leg in the crash.

1936

Private Dreams

WHAT AMBITION DOES an individual designer need to take on the might of the factories? Just the confidence that he can do it better. There have been some notable candidates.

Hybrids were always a temptation. Like the 1977 350 title-winning three-cylinder Yamaha built in the Netherlands by grafting an extra cylinder on to a 250 twin. Or the earlier home-brewed Linto, offering an alternative to the privateer singles by marrying two Aermacchi 250 racing engines together to make a twin.

Other Italians nurtured their dreams through the generations. Giuseppe Patoni's hand-built Patons spanned the four-stroke/two-stroke divide. Giancarlo Morbidelli, a cabinet-making magnate, built his own highly successful 125 GP bikes in the 1970s, then added a 250 and a 500 to his portfolio.

Another notable pioneer plundered power-boat racing for a 500cc two-stroke engine, beating the Japanese factories on to the grid with a four-cylinder. The König was made by independent New Zealand rider Kim Newcombe and engine manufacturer Dieter König, and was by far the fastest bike of 1973. Newcombe won one GP on it, but tragically died in a non-championship race at Silverstone.

Francophones fancy alternative chassis design. Generations of radically different Elf GP racers weren't strictly private, but chassis-builder Allain Chevallier was, and in the 1980s Honda lent him factory engines for his lightweights. At the same time, Swiss Claude Fior pursued unconventional front suspension ideas.

This century F1 manufacturer Ilmor privately built a MotoGP V4, but withdrew after only a couple of races; while triple champion Kenny Roberts tried from 1997 to 2005 to beat the factories, with a series of two-stroke and four-stroke projects culminating in a 990cc V5.

The factories prevail.

Left: Freddie Frith would become the first 350 World Champion in 1949. Here in this pre-war photograph the Englishman has to fettle his own bike for a race at the Sachsenring.

Right: Engineer Mario Illien co-founded the Ilmor F1 racing engine company. When Mercedes Benz bought it, Illien decided to build a MotoGP machine for 2007. The project was short-lived. Here Garry McCoy rides a prototype in 2006.

1955

Streamlining

A GRAND PRIX RACING MOTORCYCLE IS FAST and bulbous: jutting-jawed and aggressive. The goal is to cut through the air with the least resistance, at the same time taking in just enough to cool the engine and to obtain some pressurization of the intake airbox. Just enough? Yes: intakes cause drag.

When the championship began in 1949, the bikes were naked. First champion Les Graham's AJS did have the front number-plate raked back at a jaunty angle. Within five years, and mainly led by Moto Guzzi – the Italian company had its own wind-tunnel – streamlining was being taken very seriously.

The Guzzis were low and smooth: NSU had a different idea, with a wider, flatter dustbin. In the mid-1950s Norton essayed a dolphin fairing with a long proboscis out over the front wheel – the same company worked on a low-slung design with the rider in a kneeling position, although this was never raced.

Radicalism was ended when the dolphin fairing was decreed universal. Experiments continued, and a modern GP bike is fully wind-tunnel tested, rider on board, with airflow both outside and within the bodywork carefully monitored.

Winglets have appeared from time to time – first on the works Suzukis in the 1970s and in 2010 on the factory Ducatis. And disappeared again. One problem is bikes lean over to corner, whereupon down-force becomes side-force. Another is that the bikes lift their front wheels, changing the wing's angle of attack to take-off mode.

Right: DKW rider August Hobi's dustbin fairing in 1955. The design was effective for speed, but without a stabilising tail fin lacked aerodynamic balance.

Opposite: Ducati used winglets on the fairing side in 2010, but they'd disappeared one year later. Others had tried them before, to no avail.

1954

Tyres

MIKE HAILWOOD'S FAMOUS REMARK remains unforgotten. Asked what type of tyres he was using, he looked puzzled and said: "Round and black."

Today's riders wouldn't dare be so casual. As tyres became more sophisticated, a detailed understanding of their character and performance became a vital part of any rider's armoury.

The championships began with riders on ribbed front tyres and more heavily treaded rears. For privateers, they might last for several races. They were used wet or dry. But specialization came rapidly and has never stopped.

The biggest breakthrough was treadless slicks, inherited rather belatedly from drag racing, via cars. Australian Jack Findlay won the first GP on slicks (Michelins, as it happened) in 1973.

Through the next three decades tyre development leapfrogged, Dunlop vying with Michelin; Bridgestone joining in toward the end. Radial tyres came next, then a fiendishly complex witches' brew of compound materials and carcase construction.

By the new century tyres were so specialized that they were tailor-made to suit individual tracks and weather conditions on Saturday night, then shipped to the circuits on Sunday morning, ready for the race. Only for the best riders, of course. And super-sticky one-lap tyres made a spectacle of qualifying.

With expense soaring, a radical rule change came in 2009: Bridgestone became the sole MotoGP-class tyre supplier and a "one-size-fits-all" policy meant restricted numbers and just two different choices at each track, expanded only in 2014 to three front tyres only.

The "level playing field" suited some better than others.

Left: Huge advances in tyre technology have enabled Rossi and his cohorts to achieve ever-faster corner speeds.

Opposite: Tyre tuning 1954 style – a mechanic uses a file to rough up the surface of a rear tyre at the last-ever Swiss Grand Prix.

Above: For Mike Hailwood on the MV Agusta in the mid-1960s, today's 200mph-plus speeds were more than 30 mph away.

Opposite: Record speed for a MotoGP bike is 217.037 mph, on a Honda like that of Nicky Hayden, here at Indianapolis in 2008

1965

High Speed

THE BIKE WITH THE HIGHEST TOP SPEED isn't always the winner but it can help a lot.

Flat-out speeds have risen over the years by more than a third. At the birth of the championships the 500s were just about scraping towards 150mph, although the single-cylinder bikes would struggle to get within 10 or 15mph of the four-cylinder bikes.

The V8 Moto Guzzi gave the figures a real boost in the mid-1950s, with a claimed top speed better than 170mph. Getting the chance to use it was the difficulty.

Two-stroke speeds settled around 190mph for a spell, although Shinichi Itoh's NSR Honda was claimed to have broken 200mph at the Hockenheimring in 1993.

The first verified double ton, however, would have to wait for the four-strokes, when the big 990s came to town. By then, all tracks had official speed traps.

The first to do 200 was Frenchman Regis Laconi, on the operatic three-cylinder Aprilia, in practice for the Italian GP at Mugello. He clocked 200.27mph, outdone a little later the same day by Tohru Ukawa's V5 Honda: at 201.63.

Ducati set the next landmark at Catalunya in pre-season 2006 tests, in the last year of the 990s. With a stiff following wind on the 0.651-mile straight, third-longest of the year (Qatar adds a few yards, but Mugello's 0.709 is the longest), Loris Capirossi's Desmosedici GP6 was clocked at 215.9mph.

The 800s came in the next year, with the aim of reducing top speeds. Bad luck there ... in 2009 Dani Pedrosa set a new record on a Honda at Mugello, at 217.037mph. Four years later, not even the beefy new 1000s had beaten that.

1952

Dashboard

A POST-WAR RACER TUCKED INTO A CROUCH and peering over the handlebars would have a view dominated by a single round rev-counter, calibrated no further than 7,000rpm and canted over, to put the needle vertical at peak revs. In that way, it could be read at a glance.

A modern MotoGP rider has a great deal more to look at, though even less time to do so.

The temperature gauge came in the 1970s, along with water-cooling. There was little else to be measured on a two-stroke. But advancing electronics brought switchable engine-management mapping (softer power for wet weather, for example) and integrated dashboards. A digital read-out told the rider which map he was using.

The most useful addition was an automatic on-board lap-timer, triggered by a fixed beam and nowadays set to record section times, as well as a full lap.

Four-strokes and their burgeoning electronics brought complexity.

A new-century MotoGP bike now has an integrated screen, with two separate pages. The first is for the mechanics, giving detailed information on fuel pressure and temperature, oil and water temperature, oil pressure and revs.

The rider's page is simpler: revs, engine map position, gear position and temperature – switchable between water and oil. And the lap timer.

Warning lights serve when he is too busy to read the rev counter. One signals when revs reach gear-change point, the other warns of any malfunction, but in a race riders often ignore that ... until the engine stops.

In 2014, an addition allowed race officials to communicate important signals and penalties, previously relying on trackside flag signals.

Above: Yamaha rider Jorge Lorenzo can peer into the carbon-fibre tunnel in front of him to read off engine revs, water temperature, gear position, engine map setting and lap time. If he gets a moment.

Left: Bare essentials – a rider of a Moto Guzzi in 1952 had a simple white rev counter staring him in the face.

1952

Rider Clothing

UNTIL GEOFF DUKE EFFECTIVELY INVENTED one-piece leathers in 1950, riders would wear strapped jackets over leather dungarees. Like most good ideas, it seems obvious now, but Duke was the first to realize that these flapping garments caused drag and cut top speed.

A new fashion was set almost overnight and for the next 20 years there was only one way for a motorcycle racer to dress: skin-tight black leathers. Horse-hide was preferred to cow-hide, better at resisting road-rash. Kangaroo-hide is the modern option.

The design evolved to offer ever-improving protection. First it was just double-layers on knees, hips and shoulders. By the end of the 1970s, as synthetic materials developed, these were reinforced with impact-absorbing inserts. Then came back protectors, worn under the leathers, of increasingly sophisticated design.

By now, rainbow colours were the new black. Another Briton, 1970 250 champion Rodney Gould, is credited with introducing coloured leathers, daringly two-toned, and the fashion caught on. Sponsors became involved, top riders started to hire their own designers. Rossi added the variation of a contrast-colour leg in his favourite yellow. It was promptly copied in red by rival Jorge Lorenzo.

The next generation – active safety – is already with us. By 2011, both Dainese and Alpinestars had built-in airbags in their leathers, protecting neck and shoulders and triggered in milliseconds by a set of complex parameters. Those by Alpinestars can even be used twice: fall off, get on again, and it's ready once more to save you.

Right: A thin leather suit with double-skinned shoulders and a silk scarf over the chin was all the protection available to Duilio Agostini in 1952.

Opposite: Plenty friction, but the tough modern leathers saved French rider Randy de Puniet from serious road rash at Silverstone in 2010.

1953

Helmets

IF YOU HAVE A CHEAP HEAD, get a cheap helmet. The same rule applied back in 1949, when the best you could get was a pudding basin lined with webbing and cork. Riders then would be amazed at the protection offered today … and at the cost.

Early helmet research is credited to one of the doctors who treated Lawrence of Arabia (unsuccessfully) when the famed Briton sustained fatal head injuries in a road crash. By the time the championship kicked off, all riders had similar protective bowls, with goggles to protect their eyes.

That's more or less how it stayed for 20 years but for the introduction in the late 1950s of the larger "jet-style" helmet, coming down over the ears and offering the chance to replace goggles with a clip-on face shield.

The first practical full-face helmet was made in the USA for car racing in 1966. It took time to catch on in bikes: by 1971 only a handful of riders had adopted this new fashion. In spite of self-evident safety advantages, many still preferred the fresh-air feel of an open-face.

By the end of the decade, everyone was convinced.

The concept has been considerably refined in both materials and design. Carbon-fibre and Kevlar are used to reinforce the glass-fibre outer shells; sophisticated expanded plastics within provide precise impact absorption. Adjustable ventilation systems keep heads cool and visors clear. Inbuilt tubes plug into drinking systems.

Nowadays the riders' eyes are usually hidden by tinted visors. Once, you could see the whole face.

Left: Gilera rider Alfredo Milani probably felt well-protected in his pudding-basin helmet in 1953 at the Isle of Man. Nobody else had anything better.

Opposite: Aerodynamic, fully protective, comfortable, high-tech – Spanish Moto2 World Champion Toni Elias shows off a modern helmet in 2010.

Above: Black and made of leather. Nothing fancy for this 1954 racer at Assen.

Opposite: Modern boots are light and designed to be both flexible and protective. Mick Doohan tested the latter quality to the limit.

1954

Boots

A MOTORCYCLIST'S FEET NEED TO BE both active and protected from the heat of the engine, and from injury in a fall. The starting point came from the equestrian world, with knee-length cavalry boots. But the different needs meant specialized bike boots evolved from the earliest days.

Kick-starting required steel-reinforced instep, while foot pedals needed a more flexible ankle and sensitive touch than a horse-rider's stirrups even when that control was the clutch, and gears were changed by hand.

By the time of the World Championship, control conventions required even more sensitivity from the feet. One – nowadays the left, but formerly the right – operates the gear pedal; the other the rear brake. In racing, rear brake use is delicate, used to adjust cornering line and control wheelspin.

Modern boots are multi-coloured and full of technology. Micro-fibre has replaced leather; plastic guards outside and within protect against injury. Ankles are reinforced against impact while still freely hinged; Kevlar pads protect the toes at full lean.

And for the really flashy, metal inserts strike sparks as he slides along the road after falling off.

1955

Riding Style

WHICH ONE OF THESE RIDERS is about to fall off? Neither, although it may look as though Ben Spies is climbing off his Yamaha M1 in sharp contrast to Geoff Duke's neat and stylish approach to the same task of rounding a corner at maximum possible speed.

Back when tyres had tread patterns, the aim was to stay tucked in behind the fairing as much as possible to make the most of what would now be considered meagre power.

The modern style started in the 1970s – Kenny Roberts is credited as the first to drag his knee. This works as a "depth gauge" to measure the angle of lean and frequently as a crutch to regain grip when a tyre slides away.

Other riders took it further: Randy Mamola would climb so far off the inside of the bike in the 1980s that he was almost invisible.

Shifting the rider's weight inside has one big advantage: the bike becomes more upright. At a given speed it will be leaning less, which means he can raise the speed to regain maximum lean angle.

The real change was technical. Slick tyres and modern compounds gave tyres far more grip than before, making greater lean angles possible and opening the way for new techniques to exploit them.

Left: Stylish and economical, Geoff Duke set standards for neat riding. Here he tucks in on the factory Gilera at the Isle of Man in 1955. He won the race.

Opposite: Rising US star Ben Spies is nicknamed "Elbowz" for his distinctive style. He even scrapes them on the corners. He shows how at the Sachsenring in 2010.

Three

The Track

Above: The Assen weekend was always massive, and crowds in the packed grandstands got a close-up view in the 1950s.

Opposite: Oldest track on the calendar, Assen still packs them in. Nowadays the riders have a run-off area under the stands.

1953

Assen

SOME CALLED IT THE CATHEDRAL of Motorcycle Racing. Others, more aptly, the University. For fans, the Dutch TT is a midsummer festival, with upward of 100,000 filling the adjacent cow pastures with tents, motorbikes and noise.

For riders, Assen is a moody mistress, testing courage and finesse in equal measure ... and prone to sudden fits of unpredictable weather.

The oldest track still on the calendar pre-dates the World Championships and has a uniquely complex character that has been sadly and radically tamed with a major cut and rethink in 2006.

Dedicated to motorcycle racing since 1925 (only in the last 20 years have other vehicles raced there), Assen was a classic public-roads circuit. The original 18-mile loop shrunk several times, eventually settling at a more manageable 3.8 miles in 1984.

Each incarnation kept the flavour – fast corners running one into the next across the flat open countryside. Get one corner wrong, and it'd spoil your run through the next three. Or possibly deposit you and your motorcycle into one of the drainage ditches that lace the land.

It sorted out the best from the rest, then allowed them to stay close for some classic finishes, too many to list. Just think of all the great names.

It could also catch out the best: multi-champion Mick Doohan is one such famous victim of Assen injuries.

The new 2.8-mile circuit uses only a section of the old flowing Assen, and older riders mourn it still.

1973

Brno

SWEEPING WIDE AND MAJESTIC through hillsides crammed with fans, Brno is a relatively modern circuit, built in the grand old manner. This strength has given it a status in bike racing; while the challenge and variety make it an important test venue.

Not surprisingly, perhaps: for the area has a long history of motorsport, starting with the Masaryk GP on public roads in the 1930s. Parts of that track provide access to the modern purpose-built circuit, where motorcycle Grand Prix racing resumed in 1986.

In between, from 1965–82, the Czechoslovakian GP ran on a daunting 13.9-mile road track. It was cut back to 6.8 miles, but was still fearsomely dangerous for new-generation motorcycles, and after 1977 only the smaller classes continued. Sport-starved fans from behind the Iron Curtain came in hundreds of thousands.

The fine new track rejoined the calendar in 1986 as a showpiece of communism. It has outlasted the regime, with the event's name changing to Czech Republic GP in 1993.

Wide and long, it is, as Casey Stoner has observed, "one of the few tracks where you get a chance to really open up a MotoGP bike".

Brno pulls spectators from East and West to enjoy fine views of a fine track from vast natural grandstands. There are other reasons, too: the beer is not as cheap as it once was, but the night life is a good deal livelier than in the Communist days.

Left: The old Brno road course was a formidable challenge. This is 1973, and Agostini leads New Zealander Kim Newcombe's König and Englishman Chris Mortimer's "351" Yamaha.

Opposite: The modern circuit is wide, fast and enjoyable for both riders and fans. This is Nicky Hayden's Honda in 2007.

Above: All-Australian miracle. Wayne Gardner's then fiancée Donna runs on to the track to celebrate his second successive home GP win.

Opposite: Fellow-Australian Casey Stoner repeated the feat, winning from 2007 onwards. Here his Ducati is already pulling clear in 2010.

1990

Phillip Island

THIS CIRCUIT WAS MADE FOR MOTORCYCLE RACING. Some call it the Assen of the southern hemisphere. Barry Sheene called it "gateway to hypothermia". The view from across the Southern Loop across the icy Bass Strait is beautiful, but when the wind comes from up from Antarctica, it stings.

The island south of Melbourne comes alive with motorcycling at GP time. Comparisons with the Isle of Man are inevitable, and not entirely misplaced.

The track was laid out around spacious pastures by a small group including Phil Irving, renowned designer of the Vincent motorcycle. His legacy was 2.764 miles of

mainly fast and swooping corners – a track with rhythm and soul. Grand Prix racers love it. All of them.

It was first used in 1989, rewarding ecstatic fans with a thrilling home win for Wayne Gardner's Honda. Close battles were already a hallmark when Gardner won it again the next year. Then came the down time, when the raced moved to Sydney's newly-built Eastern Creek for six soulless years.

The return to the Island couldn't come soon enough: the pleasure of getting the last corner set perfect – a loop of increasingly fast left-handers on to the front straight – is unmatched. It's also the fastest track on the calendar, with a best lap at an average of 113.1mph (Lorenzo, 2013). A place you can give a MotoGP bike its head.

Spectators, wrapped up warm, get one of the best racing views in the world.

1954

Nürburgring

FEW NAMES CONJURE UP a more powerful image than the Nürburgring; no circuit demonstrates more clearly the difference between old racing and new.

The famed Nordschleife is long, fast and very dangerous – a supreme old-school motor-racing challenge. Purpose-built in the 1920s, with 160 corners in 14.2 miles, it plunges down the wooded valleys of the Eifel mountains, then soars back up to finish the lap under the brooding turret of the Nürburg Castle.

The track is still open today, still famously hard to learn, and still ready to punish mistakes severely. But it is no longer used for GP racing. The cars abandoned it first. Less politically organized, motorcycle GPs continued there, under growing protest until 1980.

Notoriously in 1974 riders led by Giacomo Agostini, Phil Read and Barry Sheene, went on strike over safety issues, leaving the race to be won by an otherwise unknown private German Yamaha: rider Edmund Czihak. His victory was his only scoring GP finish.

The track was and remains magnificent, but too deadly for Grand Prix motorbikes. The German GP moved to Hockenheim while a new modern circuit was built – safe and rather sterile, with 12 carefully profiled corners in 2.8 miles.

The bikes did go back, several times, but in 1998 the car-park circuit at the Sachsenring took over the German GP.

Above: The replacement track was tight. Here 1996 winner Luca Cadalora leads Alex Criville and Alex Barros. Champion Mick Doohan wears number 1, in fifth.

Left: The Adenau Bridge on the old long circuit in 1954 – it had 160 corners in 14.2 miles.

1950

Isle of Man TT

A PLACE OF LEGENDS, the Isle of Man was at the birth and at the heart of motorcycle racing. Legions of fans say it still is. But it was kicked off the Grand Prix calendar after 1976, first and most prominent victim of the safety lobby.

They had good grounds, too. The TT death toll up to 2010 was in excess of 200, and even with more than 100 years of it, the risks were not consistent with the growing speeds and growing status of the World Championship.

Grand Prix racing arguably lost a lot. The 37-and-three-quarter-mile Mountain Circuit dwarfs such phrases as "supreme test". With an average speed of more than 130mph on a modern production-based Superbike, a MotoGP bike would be even more breathtakingly fast.

TT specialists are a world apart from today's MotoGP riders. Dedicated to the unique thrill of racing on closed public roads, they face the risks as part of the challenge. The danger comes from the nature of the normally quiet country roads, lined with everyday objects such as telegraph poles, stone walls, trees and corner shops. Any accident at these speeds is potentially fatal.

The loss of two championship leaders in two years – 250 leader Santiago Herrero in 1970 and 125 star Gilberto Parlotti in 1972 – triggered a Spanish and Italian withdrawal; Barry Sheene, Phil Read and Giacomo Agostini then led a riders' revolt and thereafter the British GP moved to the mainland.

The TT flourished regardless, still drawing hordes of fanatical fans for a June fortnight festival of practice and what they all call "real racing".

Above: A mechanic in a flat cap prepares a blackboard to signal his rider while another bike flashes past the unique scoreboard in 1950.

Opposite: Grand Prix racing left the island in 1976. The TT continues regardless to this day, for a new breed of road-racing specialists. The fastest average more than 130mph.

1957

Spa-Francorchamps

THE SPECTACULAR BELGIAN CIRCUIT is a highlight of the F1 calendar but seems forever lost to motorcycle racing. It's probably just as well. Another classic track based on a public-road layout, the combination of ultra-fast corners with ultra-close barriers means that crashing at Spa can have very severe consequences.

Riders often have mixed feelings about such circuits. Those with the greatest objective danger are often the most enjoyable to ride: Spa is no exception.

Spa was one of six races on the founding 1949 calendar and a place of legends. Serial winners include John Surtees, Mike Hailwood and Giacomo Agostini.

The original 8.8-mile circuit was very fast indeed, and certainly by modern standards. In 1977 champion Barry Sheene won the race there on his Suzuki at an average speed of 135.067mph. It still stands as a record speed for a GP, more than 30 years later. The highest race-winning average speed in 2010 was 108.8mph at Phillip Island in Australia.

In 1979, Sheene and his fellow top riders walked out of the race on safety grounds but after a one-year interlude at Zolder, the track was resurfaced and racing resumed until 1990. The last winner there was the great champion Wayne Rainey on a factory Yamaha. The first had been British AJS rider Bill Doran, after whom a bend on the Isle of Man is named.

Right: A classic view of a classic circuit: dustbin-faired bikes started outside the pits on the left, and streamed towards the tricky Eau Rouge corner complex in 1957.

Opposite: The same stretch of track from the opposite direction. The rider is Freddie Spencer (Honda) in 1983. He finished second, but won the championship.

Above: In 1987 the race moved to Donington Park after ten years at Silverstone, and stayed there until 2009. This is first winner Eddie Lawson on the factory Yamaha.

Opposite: Back at Silverstone in 2010, and again a Yamaha won. This photograph shows eventual champion Jorge Lorenzo crossing the line.

1987

British Grand Prix

BRITAIN WAS A FOUNDING MEMBER of the World Championship, but the British GP was a late-comer. The first race was held at Silverstone, in 1977.

Until that time the British round had been held on the Isle of Man: the oldest motorcycle race meeting in the world.

Tradition was lacking but the timing was right and the venue well-suited. Not too far from London or the big cities of the Midlands, the crowds poured in to see new national hero Barry Sheene, who had already secured his second successive 500cc championship.

They were disappointed by a damp race, with Sheene and his supposed main rival Johnny Cecotto both retiring. Victory went to Pat Hennen, the first American to win a premier-class GP.

Sheene never won his home GP, but he and Silverstone were linked by fate. In 1978, timekeeping muddles robbed him of a claimed victory in streaming rain; then in 1979 he lost by inches in an unforgettable televised clash with his nemesis Kenny Roberts; and in 1982 his top-flight career was effectively ended by a big crash in pre-race practice.

From 1987 to 2009 the race moved to the parkland acres of Donington Park, rather further north, but in 2010 the GP returned to a much-revised Silverstone and to some old-timers it seemed to have come home.

1953

Track Surfaces

MANICURED TARMAC WITH CONSISTENT levels of grip for a full lap is the least modern GP riders expect, and if they don't always get this, they tend to complain. It's hard to imagine what they would have said about having to race on cobbled streets.

At the start of the championship, they had to put up with it. Indeed, with so many tracks based on public roads, the variety in surfaces depended on where you were. Cobbles in East Germany, day-to-day tarmac on the Isle of Man and elsewhere, more cobbles at Monza. And later over a railway level crossing in Finland.

The science of tyre compounding nowadays takes matters to a far higher level. At the height of their war at the turn of the century, Bridgestone and Michelin technicians would visit each track in advance and take plaster casts of the surface. Measurements of granular composition and coefficient of friction would be factored into the formulation of the rubber compound.

There are often problems where bikes share circuits with F1 cars. With big tyres and oodles of down force, the cars have such grip that under brakes they actually pull the road surface out of shape. MotoGP riders always arrive at circuits such as Montmelo outside Barcelona with some trepidation, waiting to see just how bad the roller-coaster ride will be into hard-braking corners.

It's still better than cobbles.

Left: This is purpose-built circuit Monza in Italy in 1953, and yes, those really are cobblestones.

Opposite: A modern track is grippy smooth, and expensive to keep that way. Defending champion Kenny Roberts (Suzuki) enjoys the ride at Malaysia's Sepang circuit on the third visit in 2001.

1954

Run-offs

THE SPEED MAY BE HIGHER TODAY, but nothing else has changed about the physics of a motorcycle crash. Whether bike and rider are sliding relatively safely on their sides or looping end over end, they generally leave the track at a tangent to the corner, continuing in the direction in which they were travelling before losing control. It's obvious, really.

The next obvious step, however, took many years to accomplish. In fact, the concept of making safer run-off areas was only implemented after growing complaints from car and bike racers forced circuit owners to take a different view on objective safety and rider protection.

It came at the cost of spectators, moved back from favourite trackside locations as new barriers carved out run-off areas. On the other hand, it was for their safety as well.

Conflicting needs of cars and bikes saw argument and controversy, and bike riders hurt or killed by new-fangled catch fences and solid car-catching barriers. The next phase worked in favour of both: run-off areas were extended and covered with gravel to safely slow whatever was travelling across it, car or bike.

All-time top privateer Jack Findlay once jokingly pointed out the boulders beside the access road to the new Brno circuit – part of the old track. "You see, we had gravel run-off in the old days but the stones were a bit bigger."

A trend of the new century has been to pave the first part of the run-off, giving riders a chance to lift up and recover if they enter a corner too fast.

Above: Into the "kitty litter" – Norwegian rookie Sturla Fagerhaug slides off safely at Jerez in 2010.

Left: Fall at the Hockenheim in 1954, and you might miss the crowd, but you would certainly hit a straw bale.

1955

Grandstands

CURRENT RACING FANS MIGHT THINK that the concept of a stadium circuit, like Valencia's Ricardo Tormo track, is new. Far from it. The compact layout there sets new standards, with 60,000 grandstand seats giving a view of most of the circuit and another 60,000 tiered seats on the hillsides opposite. But Valencia's crowd-rich atmosphere still doesn't compare with the old Hockenheimring, where a long and very fast track took riders way out through empty forests, then brought them back into a six-corner stadium section lined with stands and packed with up to 100,000 people.

The key was not that the bikes could be seen all the way round as at Valencia, but the opposite – they disappeared for most of the lap, then after a long minute you could hear the leaders approaching again, at almost 200mph, the sound of engines at full stretch rising and falling eerily with the combined effects of wind and Doppler.

When they burst back into view, round the corner of the first grandstand, the whole crowd would gasp at once and the riders could hear their cheers and shouts as they battled on toward the finish line.

Assen also has a classic grandstand view: overlooking not only the start and finish lines and the pits, but also the crucial final chicane, scene of frequent tooth-and-nail race finishes over the years. When the track was redesigned and another famous Assen grandstand/corner combination lost – the Strubben corner – they rebuilt a replica of it on the newer tighter track.

Above: Assen now – seats for the multitudes in 2010. But the fans in 2010 were still at the mercy of the fickle weather.

Left: Assen then – standing room only on the trackside banks for the Dutch TT in 1955.

1965

Advertising

THE FIRST WORLD CHAMPION, Les Graham, recommended Craven "A" cigarettes ("Made specially to prevent sore throats"), his balding and slightly avuncular features smiling out of print advertisements of the early 1950s in an early example of commercialization of racing. So too did British football hero Stanley Matthews – smoking was fashionable in those days.

Since that time the nowadays ill-favoured tobacco sponsors have poured many hundreds of millions into GP racing. And they would still do so, if they had not been prevented by legislation.

Early trackside banners concentrated mainly within the motorcycle trade. Ferodo brakes, Dunlop and Avon tyres, Castrol ... The winning rider's bonuses came from the same sources; Graham's cigarette contract was an exception.

For a long spell in the 1980s and beyond, it seemed that Marlboro owned the world of racing ... at least in terms of trackside banners, as they sponsored not only top riders and teams but also many race events. At least until Rothmans, Lucky Strike, Camel and other brands got in on the act.

This mother lode of money was voluntarily withdrawn by the beleaguered but still rich tobacco industry at the end of 2006 and MotoGP has struggled to replace it. Repsol and Fiat are among the handful of big players now, while Red Bull sponsored both races in the USA with striking trackside presence. On the other hand, at a rainy British GP at Donington Park in 2010, sodden fans were enjoined instead to "Visit Spain".

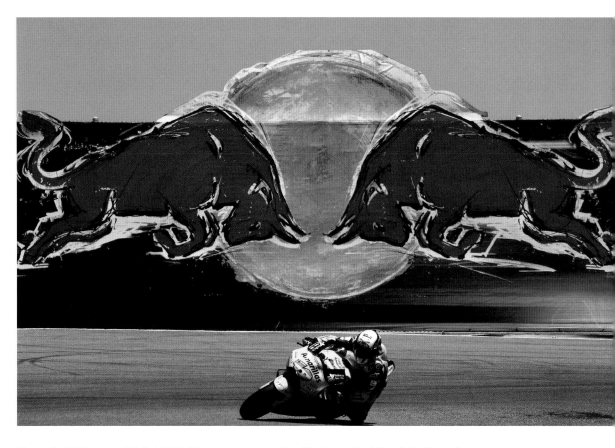

Above: By 2010, energy drink Red Bull had taken over at Laguna Seca. The banner dwarfs Ducati rider Hector Barbera.

Left: Makeshift trackside signs at the TT in 1965 are mainly for bike-trade products ... and a newspaper, but Mike Hailwood's MV is in its own livery.

1954

Crowd Protection

INSTANCES OF CRASHING MOTORCYCLES running into the crowd are mercifully rare, since the abandonment of street racing. Looking at the old pictures, it's amazing that this was not more common.

Crowd control was rudimentary at best even at the better circuits, where "prohibited areas" marked out the more obviously dangerous locations. But at the far reaches of the championship – at the old Sachsenring in East Germany, at Opatija in Yugoslavia and Imatra in Finland – the tracks were too long or their surroundings too difficult for such measures, and crowds lined the very edges of the track at some points.

This remains true today only at the surviving public-roads events – mainly at the Isle of Man, in Ireland and at scattered points in Eastern Europe.

Crowds are now safely distanced. A more modern worry, with higher speeds and the influence of gravel traps, is that cartwheeling motorcycles have been known to clear trackside barriers. Valentino Rossi crashed in practice at Valencia and his Yamaha looped right over the Armco and the adjacent service road. It was not an area with crowd access, but at Misano in 2007, in a non-GP event, one bike went over the bales and bounced over two fences to land in the grandstand. Fortunately, it was empty.

Above: Crowds are perilously close as Hans Baltisberger swoops past on his 250 NSU (in its "duckbill" phase) at the Hockenheimring in 1954.

Opposite: When winner Jorge Lorenzo went to greet his home crowd at Montmelo in Catalunya, he first had to cross a gravel trap before he could lean against the Airfence. And they were still three fences away.

1954

Scoreboards

NOWHERE BEFORE OR SINCE has equalled the Isle of Man for having a picturesque scoring system. Rooted in the origins of the event before World War One, the massive scoreboard had a clock hand which detailed the progress of every competitor as he passed certain key points on the circuit; while his race time, communicated by telephone, was chalked beneath by a team of uniformed boy scouts.

Since riders were out of sight for half an hour or so, this spectacle was the only entertainment for the fans in the facing grandstands, who otherwise saw precious little action aside from pit stops.

Electronics finished the boy-scout era. In any case, a modern Grand Prix lap seldom lasts much more than 90 or 100 seconds. All circuits now use giant TV screens to monitor the action, so the bikes are never out of sight. Riders in the lead often use these screens as a sort of rear-view mirror, checking the image to see what's behind them.

Most tracks still have a tower at the start line, showing the racing numbers of the leading riders, but for professionals in the pits and paddock there is a wealth of detail available on a series of screens. Banks of monitors show race positions and lap times; a rider's real-time position on the track, section times and more. You can follow the whole race without looking at the track once.

More was to follow with the flowering of technology. A plethora of information has become available on tablets and smart-phones: this includes timing, race monitoring and a choice of camera views.

Right: Boy scout volunteers were employed to keep tabs on 50 or more riders at the Isle of Man TT in 1954.

Opposite: All the timing details at the click of a channel-changer. By 2010 fans could follow live timing and position tracking on mobile telephones.

1950

Starting Grid

IT GOES WITHOUT SAYING that the atmosphere on the starting grid is like nothing else. The tension has stayed the same over the years, but also radically altered. With clutch starts having replaced dead-engine push starts in 1987, pre-race silence has been drowned out by revving engines.

Different tracks had different numbers on a grid row in the early days ... depending on width you could have up to eight front-row starters. Since they all would get their engines going at slightly different times, overcrowding at the first corner was seldom a problem, at least at the front.

By the 1980s standardization was coming in: four-man grid rows became the norm until 2006; then in 2007 a new three-rider grid pattern was adopted for the premier class only, eventually adopted by all in 2011.

Grids were still places for doing the business of racing. Mechanics would fuss around the bikes until the last minute, then push their riders off for the warm-up lap. With commercialization, a new kind of business joined in: TV business.

By the new century, the pre-race show accommodated the fans at home. Riders would complete the sighting lap, then take their grid slots, switch off ... and then must remove their helmets. In this way the cameras could roam around, and in rare cases might even get a word with the rider.

It's a relief to them when the signal comes to clear the grid. Mechanics start the engines, the riders snap down their visors ... and soon the real work of the day will begin.

Above: Blast-off for 6,000 horsepower ... MotoGP riders, pole qualifier Pedrosa in the foreground, launch at Mugello at the 2013 Italian GP. Lorenzo, half-hidden, will win.

Left: Awaiting the start of the Lightweight (250) TT in 1950. Uniquely, Isle of Man races started riders in pairs at ten-second intervals. They raced the clock, not each other. Winner, by two tenths of a second, was Dario Ambrosini (Benelli, 96).

1954

In the Pit Garage

WHERE ONCE MECHANICS might consider themselves lucky to have enough shelf space to store their tools and an umbrella if it rained hard, the top tracks now offer spacious pit boxes, some with toilets and showers. Within these spaces, liveried fold-away partitions are erected to create workspace for the growing group of electronics experts, for team management and others and sometimes a viewing gallery for VIP guests.

For years racing bikes were relatively low-maintenance, especially the privateer machines. Factory squads aside, top riders would generally have just one mechanic and maybe a helper, and would expect to get their own hands dirty once in a while.

But the complexities of a modern MotoGP bike dictate a platoon of specialists to keep it in top fettle. Honda rider Dani Pedrosa's pit is typical: his crew chief commands five mechanics, with one electronics engineer, one factory technician and one suspension expert standing by. Add a tyre man and (shared between riders) a manager, a coordinator and a spare-parts controller, and you're ready to go racing.

The atmosphere in the pits can hardly have changed much, whether indoors or out. It's a "chuck-me-a-spanner" mateyness forged through miles of travel and late-night rebuild sessions.

Perhaps it's not as chummy as it once was, though. During his spell with Yamaha, Valentino Rossi pioneered a wall down the middle of the pit. Ostensibly this was because they were on different makes of tyre, but significantly when that difference was eliminated the next year, Rossi's pit wall stayed.

Left: Final checks for the factory NSU machines at the Ulster GP in 1954.

Opposite: Crew chief Juan Martinez and rider Nicky Hayden confer briefly in the pit. Ducati mechanics stand by with the mobile starter motor on the right.

1981

Before the Race

ASKED WHAT GOES THROUGH THEIR MINDS before a race, different riders give different answers. Freddie Spencer scoffed at the idea of pre-race nerves. "That's show-time!" he insisted. Others will admit that the hardest part is waiting for the start.

Barry Sheene, mid-1970s superstar, found that smoking one of his untipped French cigarettes helped ease the tension and he had a hole drilled in his full-face helmet so he could puff away until the last minute.

The most competitive riders treat those moments as part of the race. It's a last chance to gain a psychological advantage over your nearest rivals. A quick dubious glance at his tyre might unsettle him; privateer 350 World Champion Jon Ekerold (1980) told me how he went over and gave French rival Patrick Fernandez a hug before the start of his home GP. "I said: 'The tension must be terrible, Patrick' – and I felt him shudder."

A modern grid would not lend itself to such an exchange. Riders sit in a world of their own, helmets off only because it's the TV-friendly rule. Nicky Hayden listens to hip-hop; others prefer rock. Umbrella girls stand and smile; mechanics stand by with tyre warmers and starting mechanisms, crew chiefs defend the territory.

Valentino Rossi still preserves his long-time ritual, however. He genuflects to the bike, holds the footrest, creating a mental barrier between real life and the race to come.

Left: All-time Spanish star Angel Nieto adjusts his helmet before the 125cc GP at Jarama in Spain in 1981. He won the race on his Minarelli, and the championship – one of 13.

Right: Tyres wrapped up warmly; race-face on, Marc Marquez is a study in concentration at Motegi in Japan in 2013. Regulations require riders to remove their helmets for the TV cameras.

1959

After the Race

IT'S A STRANGE MOMENT, after it is all over. Two (in the old days three) days of practice and adjusting the bike, two nights of tension, and all the pre-race nerves have culminated in 45 minutes of sheer concentration of effort and maximum risk. No wonder riders, already exhausted, sometimes feel suddenly deflated.

But there are formalities to be completed, congratulations to be accepted, and prizes to be waved aloft.

The physical effort is tremendous. Riders lose weight during a race, even while replenishing fluid from back-packs in their leathers. It's not that unusual for a rider to finish a race in a state of physical collapse.

But it seems today's generation don't know how easy they have it.

The average modern MotoGP race lasts for 45 minutes. When the series began in 1949 it was very different. The shortest of six races lasted well over an hour: 32 laps of Monza at an average speed of 98.105mph took winner Nello Pagani 1h 16'36.8 (second-placed Gilera team-mate Arciso Artesiani took just eight tenths of a second longer).

The longest race was the TT. Winner Harold Daniell battled the Isle of Man Mountain Circuit for an epic three hours, at 3h 02'18.6.

Left: Drenched and shattered, 1959 Senior TT winner John Surtees needed his hands massaging before he could grasp the trophy. The race had lasted three hours.

Right: Italian Luca Cadalora is exhausted by intense effort in intense heat at Shah Alam in 1996. The Honda-mounted winner had raced for less than 47-and-a-half minutes.

1954

Transporters

DID RIDERS REALLY used to sleep under their trucks, so the bikes could stay warm and dry inside? The tales are legion among the old-timers but it is certainly true that for the first 20 or 25 years the vast bulk of competitors, privileged factory runners apart, shared their accommodation with their motorcycles.

The lucky ones might have a long-wheelbase van, making life a little less cramped. It was only in the late 1960s that caravans came into vogue but it was still a case of hitching up to your bike transporter to get there.

Nowadays even small teams in the smaller classes have a dedicated transporter, while a respectable factory team has two 17-metre truck-trailers units drawn up behind the pit. At some tracks, the tractor units are assembled at an adjacent car park, a colourful display in themselves.

Inside are offices and meeting rooms, and combined storage for transporting the bikes with work benches, as well as somewhere for the rider to change out of his leathers.

Assembling these vehicles in the crowded paddock is an art perfected by teams' association IRTA, leading to the cruel nickname of "Captain Car Park" for General Secretary Mike Trimby. It remains an impressive logistical feat as time-lapse sequences of the paddock coming together each weekend clearly show.

Left: In a poignant picture, the covered wreckage of Dennis Lashmar's Pike-BSA lies next to his sign-written transporter, after his fatal crash at Solitude in the 1954 German GP.

Opposite: Modern MotoGP teams plough many hundreds of thousands into their sophisticated transporters.

Above: Poised to push – Geoff Duke (left, Gilera) is joined by Walter Zeller and guest rider John Surtees (both BMW) and Carlos Bandirola on the fully faired MV Agusta at the Nürburgring in 1955.

Opposite: Max Biaggi, multiple 250 champion, is pushed into life by a mechanic during practice. His Aprilia is a two-stroke: modern four-strokes are harder to fire up.

1955

Push Starts

FROM 1949 TO 1986 ALL GRAND PRIX races started with dead engines. From 1987 onward, the tradition was abandoned. Under the influence of a new generation of American riders, a clutch start was introduced.

It was fairer, in that a fast qualifier did not risk losing all his advantage, should his bike prove reluctant to fire up. And it introduced a new element: the sound of frantically revving engines, while riders' eyes strained, looking for the first twitch of the starter's flag.

But it also meant something quite unique had been lost: that deathly silence as the seconds ticked down to the start, then the patter of feet before one, then two and then all of the engines burst into life.

Run-and-bump starting procedure was a ritual: prime the carburettor, pull back against compression, declutch, then lean as hard as you can on the front brake, tensed like a spring, awaiting the moment of release.

Nowadays lights have replaced the man with the flag; while a judge watches each row (up to 13 in the Moto2 class) to check that nobody goes too early.

Just as well they no longer have to do the old run-and-bump. A modern MotoGP bike has a special one-way slipper clutch, putting the task somewhere between "difficult" and "impossible".

Four
The People

1955

Lady Racers

A STARTING GRID MAY BE no place for a lady, but there have been a select few who have broken the rules. And for a spell, they really were rules – put in place specifically to forbid females in GP racing.

The first notable challenge came from Britain in 1961, from housewife Beryl Swain. She entered the 50cc TT, a championship event, only to be told she was below the hitherto notional minimum weight limit. Swain ate herself fat and raced, to 22nd place but when she applied to go GP racing the next year, the FIM responded with a "no girls" rule.

It lasted until excised by the growing movement for women's liberation in time for the next fast lady: the wispily pretty Taru Rinne from Finland. She rode in the 125 class of 1988 and 1989, by the end of which a bad crash cut her career short. But she had impressed: a best result of seventh and 17th overall was very respectable.

So too was the next girl racer: Tomoko Igata from Japan. She equalled a best of seventh in her two-year run in the mid-1990s, also on a 125. At the time this was a highly competitive series and a top-ten finish no mean feat.

The next fair maiden to try her luck was blonde beauty Katja Poensgen. The German daughter of a motorcycle-trade magnate, Katja rode a 250 in the 2001 season. She only scored points once, finishing 14th in Italy, but again she made a strong enough fist of it to shrug off any girly taunts.

More than ten years later, potential replacements were few and far between.

Right: Sidecar passenger Ingeborg Stoll-Laforge was a woman racer before any solo riders, from 1952. Inge was killed in a non-championship race at Brno in 1958.

Opposite: Indistinguishable from her male rivals with her visor down, Katja Poensgen ran a 250 campaign in 2001.

1956

Grid Girls

SMILING DUTIFULLY, the brolly dollies are an integral part of a Grand Prix grid. The aim is two-fold: to shade the rider or keep him dry, and to draw the lenses of the scurrying photographers.

A few riders' wives jealously guard the role for themselves. In more than one case, that is where they met.

The first professional grid girls were chaste-looking maidens in national dress. How things have changed.

Back at the beginning, wives and girlfriends seldom joined the very male gathering in the minutes before a race. It was not until the 1970s or later that grid girls outnumbered mechanics as the riders' last-minute companions.

That had been in the friendly pre-commercial pre-TV times, when there were no brands to be promoted nor logos to be displayed.

Nowadays professional models or, often as not, enthusiastic amateurs fill the role and some teams even include grid girls on the permanent payroll, while the liveries vie to be more eye-catching and revealing. Except in strait-laced Qatar, where the aim is the opposite.

Is the glamour incongruous? Or just part of the sport?

Racing would certainly be less exciting without them.

Left: A chaste kiss on the cheek from a girl in national costume for Geoff Duke, after victory in the Swedish GP of 1956.

Opposite: Nothing chaste in the suggestive uniforms of new-century grid girls, working in packs to hunt down the photographers.

1978

Celebrities

BIKE RACING ATTRACTS ALL SORTS including kings and other royalty. In America, this category might include sundry media or Hollywood stars – Brad Pitt is a Laguna Seca regular, Tom Cruise a grid walkabout man, while TV talk-show host Jay Leno played the role of Grand Marshal (whatever that means) at Indianapolis in 2010, waving the chequered flag at the winner.

But in Spain, it's rather different. There, a king really is just that. King Juan Carlos is a big bike-racing fan and a Grand Prix regular, and even intervened in a spat between head-to-head rivals Jorge Lorenzo and Dani Pedrosa, who were playing no-speaks at the time.

British royalty has dabbled in bike racing but seldom, although Prince George, Duke of Kent, was a pre-war fan and became the first Royal to visit the Isle of Man TT in the 1930s. In the new century, Prince Harry makes up for it. Both he and his brother William are keen motorcyclists and private track-day fans, and in 2009 Harry took a fast lap as passenger to Randy Mamola on the GP Ducati two-seater at the British GP.

Sundry pop singers come and go, but no one could beat the celebrity brought along by Barry Sheene: Beatle George Harrison was, after all, so close to royalty in the 1970s that kings themselves paid homage.

Right: Racing fan and former Beatle George Harrison relaxes with British champion Barry Sheene at Brands Hatch in 1978.

Opposite: Top guns – Hollywood star Tom Cruise shakes hands with bike-racing star Nicky Hayden (Honda) before the 2008 US GP.

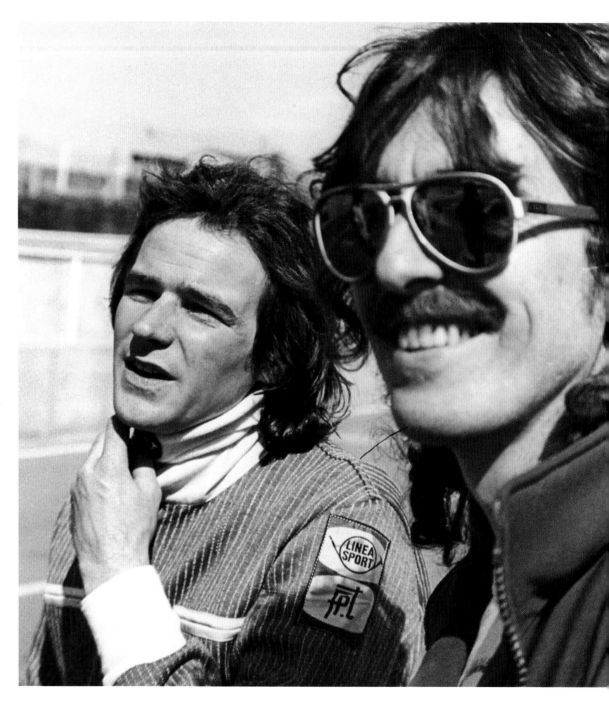

1963

Vantage Points

RACING FANS WILL PUT UP WITH A LOT in exchange for a good view: close enough to feel the noise, but taking in enough track to follow the action.

Some of the best are artificial: grandstands at Assen overlooked the crucial final chicane and finish line; at Valencia some seats show the whole circuit.

Others are natural. Brno has one of the best: a symmetrical curve of hillside overlooking four corners, two of them at the viewers' feet. Jerez is ringed with suitably steep hills. Phillip Island offers trackside banks with long views. Laguna Seca's Corkscrew is a fascinating tight spot: close and dramatic, with views over the far side of the little track as well.

Nowhere did fans get closer than on the Isle of Man. On the mountain section of the 37 ¾ miles, they could, if they wished, hang their legs over the trackside wall.

Still more great vantage points are reserved for privileged passholders. France's Paul Ricard circuit had a long straight and at the end of it a guard rail, where riders and paddock people would gather to watch the thrilling sweep that followed.

But some of the best were strictly do-it-yourself.

Spa-Francorchamps had one particular giant advertising hoarding overlooking the Eau Rouge corner complex. Fans climbed up the support structure, then cut holes through the signboard for an exclusive view.

And at the Sachsenring, there was an informal private competition as to who could build the tallest teetering tower.

Left: Bring your own timber, build your own grandstand. East German fans at the Sachsenring in 1963 were used to making do after years behind the Iron Curtain.

Right: The long view at green and pleasant Donington Park in 2009.

Showing Your Colours

SUPREME RACER AND MARKETING GENIUS Valentino Rossi made it simple for his fans to show their colours. He made them just one colour: yellow. This now effectively belongs to him in the same way as lime green belongs to racing Kawasakis.

Riders had their fans, of course, from the dawn of the Championship. When their heroes all wore black leathers and white helmets, the fans tended to look the same too.

There were always amiable eccentrics, like Britain's Union Jack-wearing self-styled "Superfan" of the 1970s: clothing and headgear adorned with badges and stickers of tribute.

Fan fashion took off when commercial sponsors came in. Barry Sheene fans would wear Texaco jackets; other distinctive race-team designs quickly took hold and the clothing manufacturers didn't take long to catch on.

Soon the scale of the growing industry demanded control and today officially licensed clothing concessions ring the race-track entrances and clones of every factory team on the grid are well represented in the stands. And in the airports on the flights home the next day.

It was the Rossi fans who first got organized, with the fan club block-booking grandstands at his home race at Mugello and everybody in them wearing yellow. Rival of the 500cc days Max Biaggi followed suit in red, matching his Marlboro Yamaha sponsorship. His grandstands were slightly smaller: today Ducati has inherited the sponsorship, the colour and a rather larger all-red grandstand at another Mugello corner.

Above: Fans of Valentino Rossi coordinate their hero worship at the Malaysian GP at the Sepang International circuit in 2010. Shuffle them around, and they'd still spell "trouble" for his rivals.

Left: This fan's hat of 1965 may be rough and ready, but it shows a true petrol head ... there's even a gauge to check the level.

Right: Mechanics watch and wait in the pits at Assen in 1953. Nothing separates them from the track.

Opposite: A win for the rider is a win for all. A Rossi crewman punches the air as the rider equals Giacomo Agostini's record of 68 premier-class wins at Misano in 2008.

1953

The Race Crew

EVERY TEAM NEEDS A TEA-BOY, a driver, a wheel-cleaner, fairing fitter, sprocket changer, brake man, gopher ... In the 1950s it was often as not the same person – And those weren't his only duties.

There has never been any shortage of volunteers to get their hands dirty. Once a private rider's crew might be an old school friend or a racing chum good with the spanners. Now a top factory team's pit will have 15 or 20 professionals in it full time and even a single-rider satellite team needs a crew of eight or nine.

The job's appeal is more than sharing the pleasure of the travel, the glamour of the racing. As riders well know, racing is very much a team effort. And it was even before every squad had a separate staff man to see to each of the tasks named above.

Factory teams of the early days would wear matching overalls; most of the rest were scruffy or smart according to temperament. Modern mechanics, even in the lowliest 125 teams, all have liveries and logos.

There's a special bond within a team. Everybody shares the same tension during a race, when all their work is done and only the rider matters. Will something on the bike fail? Will it be his responsibility? Nobody wants to let the crew down.

And when their man crosses the line first, it really is a victory for everyone.

144

1939

Race Officials

THERE HAS BEEN A RADICAL SHIFT from what became known as the bad old days of officialdom.

Grand prix racing was sanctioned from the outset by the Geneva-based Fédération Internationale de Motocylisme (FIM). This was borne in 1949, by no coincidence the same year as the World Championships, out of a much earlier federation based in Britain.

The FIM was an amateur body and soon gained a reputation for governing the sport in an amateurish and autocratic way. Personified by a local representative in a blue blazer with a special arm-band, crucial decisions were often inconsistent and the organization suffered badly from slow-response inertia.

The reputation lingered perhaps unfairly after action by the riders – and a threatened breakaway independent World Series – forced the FIM to improve its methods. There were also many individuals, such as the Swiss Luigi Brenni, head of the road-race commission in the 1970s and 1980s, who offered a willing ear and a voice of reason.

But it was all turned upside down in 1992, when Dorna leased the commercial rights from the FIM and introduced hard-core professionalism. The FIM retained a sporting role, but its officials were now permanent employees rather than sundry local chieftains.

Today FIM officials work hand-in-glove with Dorna and the teams' association, IRTA. But in terms of real power, the boot is clearly now on the other foot.

Left: In a quaint TT tradition on the Isle of Man in the 1950s, helmets were passed fit for use and then impounded until the rider went out on track. Official Len Attwood was the keeper of the heads.

Right: Signs of the times: an official carries warning boards to show riders before the start of the 2010 Portuguese GP.

1954

Famous Team Bosses

THERE COULD HAVE BEEN NO GREATER CONTRAST between the glamorous four-cylinder Italian Gileras and the simple single-cylinder factory Nortons, which vied for supremacy in the early championship years. Nor between their respective team bosses.

Gilera was run by the equally glamorous Piero Taruffi, Grand Prix driver, record-breaker, designer and author – known as the "Silver Fox" for his mane of white hair.

Norton was headed up by Ulsterman Joe Craig, with his ascetic appearance and taciturn manner. Dour and old-fashioned, his motorcycles were much the same.

MV Agusta was an offshoot of the Agusta family aviation company, founded by Count Vincenzo and his brother Domenico Agusta. Both were passionate about racing and after Vincenzo's death in 1958, Domenico maintained a presence in the dominant team's pits.

Walter Kaaden is famous for his pioneering work on high-performance two-strokes. Equally impressive was the fact that the MZ team boss did it on a shoe-string budget from the East German firm. In sports coat, tie and hat, Kaaden was a distinctive figure.

Glamour seems to be lacking in the modern era. Honda's most notable racing chief was Youichi Oguma of the 1980s. Austere appearance masked a sense of humour and a devastating authority.

Team chiefs nowadays are businessmen rather than aristocrats. The days of big personalities seem far away.

Right: Austere Norton chief Joe Craig talks to rider Ray Amm on the grid at Solitude in Germany in 1954.

Opposite: Honda's top brass join riders Nicky Hayden (left) and Dani Pedrosa (far right) for the team launch. From left, HRC President Suguru Kanazawa, Honda Motor President Takeo Fukui and HRC MD Satoru Horiike. All had worked together in the race team in the 1970s and beyond.

2006 Honda Racing

1953

Race Marshals

RAIN OR SHINE, THEY'RE OUT THERE: a volunteer force without whom none of this would be possible. Race marshals. The guys who signal the riders, monitor everything, and pick up the pieces when it all falls apart.

From time immemorial, this has been an amateur's job and in the early days marshals at lesser-used circuits often lacked experience. At some of the longer tracks, the distance between corners – and thence marshal posts – was often considerable. The Isle of Man dealt with this uniquely: travelling marshals on motorcycles. Often ex-racers, this squad could be rapidly mobilized so that each marshal rides to the next marshal post, covering the full circuit in one sweep. If one did not turn up at the next post, this located where an incident might have taken place out of sight.

The revolution in racing safety has seen standards rise: marshals at the major circuits are numerous, experienced and well-drilled. With up to 30 at each post, a GP has 240 to 260 of them. At new circuits where local experience is lacking, such as in Qatar and Turkey, old hands from other circuits are shipped in to supervize.

Each post is in radio contact with race control; communication is constant.

They still run into trouble: in 2011 Jerez marshals were accused of favouritism toward Rossi after he had knocked Stoner down. Although later exonerated, the incident threw a focus on the question of the marshals' responsibilities. In motorcycling, unlike car racing, they are allowed to help a competitor restart ... but not compelled to do so: their own safety comes first.

Left: Marshals, reporters and fans wait expectantly on the Isle of Man in 1953.

Opposite: Casey Stoner corners hard at the Sachsenring in 2010. Up to 30 marshals at a corner are there to pick up the pieces.

1954
Designers

LANDMARK DESIGNS COME from landmark designers. Even unsuccessful designs can be instructive but the best continue to influence today's racing and road motorcycles.

First on the roll of honour is Piero Remor. His first-ever twin-cam transverse four-cylinder engine came before World War II, but his designs would dominate GP racing from 1952 to 1974 with Gilera and MV Agusta, and keep on returning, on both road and track.

Contemporary Giulio Carcano designed simple twins and singles for Moto Guzzi, but his supreme moment came with the 500cc V8 of the late 1950s: an extravagance yet to be repeated.

Elsewhere in Italy Fabio Taglioni was founding Ducati's desmo dynasty. His first 1957 desmodromic engine (positive-closing valve gear allowing higher revs) was a 125 single. Taglioni also laid down the company's trademark 90-degree V-twin design, doubled-up for MotoGP's new-century Desmosedici V4: designed, including its updated desmodromics, by current resident genius, Filippo Preziosi.

East Germany's Walter Kaaden worked alone at impoverished MZ. His unique understanding of resonance and harmonics led him to turn the workaday two-stroke into a razor-sharp racer. Using his technology and starting with Suzuki in 1962, two-strokes took over racing until they were phased out by new rules from 2002.

Soichiro "Pops" Honda was a leading light in a new Japanese generation, generally working by committee. More recently, Masao Furusawa of Yamaha had the big idea of turning a compact in-line four into a virtual V4, using a cross-plane crankshaft and bringing Piero Remor's design to the winner's circle once again.

Left: Two-stroke genius Walter Kaaden (left) in 1954, with a rotary-valve IFA motorcycle (the previous name of the MZ factory).

Right: Ducati's engineering director Filippo Preziosi is in conference with Valentino Rossi prior to the 2011 season.

1959

Mechanics

UNSUNG HEROES, grease-monkeys and experts: you don't last long in GP racing if you're not good at your job and wrenching for a top team is an ambition for all of them.

It's an ambition often exceeded, for many mechanics have become famous in their own right. They all started the same way.

MV Agusta's Arturo Magni was the prototype. He joined MV in 1950 from rival Gilera as chief mechanic to the racing team and stayed there through years of glory until the factory quit in 1977. Magni's name assured a future, converting MV road bikes into replica racers, nowadays with Moto Guzzi.

Erv Kanemoto, technical alter ego to Freddie Spencer in the early 1980s, is another name that became famous; like Kel Carruthers (Roberts and Lawson) and Nobby Clark (Mike Hailwood and others).

There's a whole army of others, stretching back to 1949. Back then they worked in primitive conditions, with simpler motorcycles. Today, they are specialists, in relative luxury.

Then and now, they would come to know their motorcycles intimately. The hallmark of the best of them is plain to see, in fast but unhurried work.

None of them, in any era, is a stranger to working through the night – especially with a crash-prone rider on their bike.

But that's part of the down side of having the perfect job.

Opposite: A Honda mechanic squats with the rider at the Japanese machine's international racing debut on the Isle of Man in 1959.

Left: Repsol Honda mechanics work with practised skill on Andrea Dovizioso's factory RC212V in 2009.

Above: So what's wrong with plain silver? John Surtees's factory MV Agusta carries a modest nose flash in 1956.

Opposite: Hardly space for one more: Stefan Bradl's LCR Honda is a patchwork of sponsor logos, sometimes changing race by race.

1956

Liveries

PIN-STRIPING WAS ALL THE RAGE when Les Graham's AJS won the inaugural championship of 1949. AJS favoured gold stripes on black, BMW white on black, Norton broader black stripes on silver. The Moto Guzzis were different: anti-corrosion treatment coloured their aluminium fairings a dull matt green. They looked unique.

One way or another, looks have always mattered in racing. German designers for NSU favoured a functional bare aluminium look for a variety of body shapes in the mid-1950s.

The liberation of colours came gradually. The dustbin-faired Gileras of the first years were in sharp two-tone: red and white. Ten years later, in 1967's epic title battle between Agostini's MV Agusta and Hailwood's Honda, the bikes were still basically two-tone and each in a slightly different combination of red and silver.

Suddenly in the 1970s things got stripy. Then came those yellow Yamahas with the broken broad-black stripe. Ridden to victory by Kenny Roberts in 1978, they established a visual brand identity that has served ever since.

Rival Barry Sheene's Suzukis displayed sponsor's livery: Texaco, in his winning years. Then came the cigarette brands: Rothmans, Lucky Strike, Marlboro and many more, each with its own brand identity to stamp on the bikes. Today, the sponsors call the tune. They decide the colour, from Marlboro's crimson to Repsol's rising-sun orange, by way of Movistar Yamaha's green Monster-flashed blue.

1952
Media

THE PRESS ROOM ON SUNDAY NIGHTS is no place for the faint-hearted. Upward of 200 journalists hunched over lap-tops, striving to dispatch their tit-bits and stories faster than the next man. Photographers, 70 or more, likewise with their all-electronic images. Websites world-wide hungrily devour every phrase: next day's newspapers formalize it in print, next week's magazines make sense of it all. Everyone is on deadline.

It was ever thus, but he difference between then and now is not how much tighter the deadlines have become, but how quickly the information is published: instantly, on the Web.

There were just a handful of permanent press-men in the early days. All knew one another and they were on first-name terms with the riders.

They'd file copy to newspapers and weekly magazines by telephone, occasionally by telex; monthly journalists might even use express post.

Today's generation types it up and clicks "Send".

How about the first-name terms? Sometimes yes. But except for the specialist core, contact today is generally in a press conference, a group meeting, and the occasional supervized one-on-one interview.

As Valentino Rossi discovered as a young rider, bitten once too often by the newspapers: "The journalists do not come here to be your friend."

Right: Denis Jenkinson (DSJ) became famous as a Formula One correspondent over many years, but he started on bikes, and won the inaugural 1949 Sidecar World Championship as a passenger.

Opposite: The Sachsenring media centre in 2010 has much in common with NASA mission control in Houston.

1954

Photographers

WHEN THE SERIES WAS BORN IN 1949, the handful of professional photographers at a Grand Prix had access to points that the modern generation can only dream about. They could stand by the trackside with little thought of the danger – on a straw bale, even.

Indeed, they needed all the help they could get. Heavy cameras with slow lenses needed plates or magazines changing frequently; film was expensive. Each shot was invaluable, anticipation was everything; every opening of the shutter must count.

How different now. Gangs of photographers, 15 or 20 strong, are confined to much more limited areas, but telephoto lenses make up for the distance, autofocus can help out the bleary-eyed and electronic cameras can shoot off 10 frames a second. Film cost? No such thing: interchangeable memory cards are able to store an unlimited number of high-resolution publication-quality frames.

The glory years for photographers were in the 1970s and 1980s, when improving cameras and lenses from Japan, as well as better colour film technology opened up all sorts of possibilities for a generation of creative snappers.

Nowadays their numbers have trebled and images are posted on the internet within minutes of being captured.

It's easier nowadays to take lots of pictures, but it's no easier to take really good ones.

Left: Photo finish – it's a close one for the lucky photographers standing by the Assen trackside in 1954. Nobody would be allowed there today.

Opposite: Clattering shutters: it's a sound that follows Valentino Rossi wherever he goes.

1953

Medical Support

THE LAST THING A RIDER WANTS TO SEE as he exits a corner at speed is an ambulance parked in front of him, back doors open wide. But that's what confronted Italian 250 champion Luca Cadalora in Sweden in the 1980s, where another rider had fallen a minute or so earlier.

He managed to miss going headfirst into the waiting stretcher but it illustrates how rudimentary medical attention could be, even in the Championship's fourth decade.

Services were laid on by volunteer groups, while only a few tracks had well-equipped medical facilities.

Compare that to 2010, when mobile trackside resuscitation was employed in a tragically unsuccessful attempt to save the life of Moto2 rider Shoya Tomizawa at Misano. Seconds after he and two other riders had fallen, two doctors were by his side.

The greatest contribution has come from another source, founded by the now-legendary Italian Dr Claudio Costa. The Clinica Mobile travels to all races, working in tandem with track medics and helping not only with crash victims but also providing rehabilitation.

It was not always easy. After a major crash at the Salzburgring in 1977, in which Swiss rider Hans Stadelman died and several more, including World Champions Johnny Cecotto, Dieter Braun and Franco Uncini were badly injured, Clinica doctors were prevented from assisting due to local laws.

Opposite: An elegant coach-built ambulance waits for customers by the trackside at Schotten for the 1953 West German GP.

Left: Doctor already in attendance, Hector Barbera is stretchered away after a tumble in practice in Australia in 2009. He was back for the 250 race the next day.

1977

Rider Groupies

FAST GIRLS HAVE ALWAYS hung around fast racers. So, have times changed? The motorcycles have got faster, but the girls probably just more numerous – while the advent of the riders' motor-homes from the 1980s created opportunities for instant romance that weren't there before.

At the same time, the testosterone-charged racers living life close to the edge are highly active in pursuit.

Stories of wild parties, all unprintable, abound from the heyday of the racing playboys in the 1960s and 1970s. And it wasn't much different on the US dirt-tracks, where a new generation of GP stars was on the move.

Nowadays, paddock life is relatively restrained: early-to-bed athletes at work don't carouse as they used to: motor-home life is more austere. Or at least that's how it looks.

And the groupies? They might be younger now, they might be banished from the pits, but the more things change, the more they stay the same.

Right: Racing's first international celebrity Barry Sheene was a glamour magnet. The beauty queens soon gathered.

Opposite: It's Shanghai in 2005, and Chinese Valentino Rossi fans march past in highly disciplined regiments.

Five

The Racing

Right: Close to touch-down – Aleix Espargaro flies his Pramac Ducati alongside the kerb at Catalunya in 2010.

Above: Phil Read (left) and Rodney Gould on near-identical Yamahas fight for second place at the Sachsenring in 1971. Gould won the battle, Read the title.

Opposite: Touching distance – Jorge Lorenzo (Yamaha) finds a way inside Casey Stoner's Ducati to win in Valencia in 2010.

1971

Overtaking

MOTORCYCLES, SLENDER AND MANOEUVRABLE, are made for overtaking in so many different ways. Classically it's in the slipstream, then cut underneath to outbrake into the corner. But there's also round the outside, the block-pass, selling him a dummy. Or just plain elbows.

At GP level, it gets harder. Machines and riders are closely matched, whether they be booming Manx Nortons of the 1950s or yowling MotoGP four-strokes in 2011. When it's like this, a rider must be more creative. Or more forceful, and usually both.

Hand-to-hand combat was seldom finer than in the early years of the Japanese factories in the mid-1960s. Honda, Yamaha and Suzuki, fought it out in the design rooms with ever-more complex machines; riders such as Phil Read, Bill Ivy, Jim Redman and Mike Hailwood did it on track. With the smooth cornering lines of the time, it was graceful and brutal.

Another highlight came in Kevin Schwantz–Wayne Rainey battles from 1988 to 1993. They would try anything to get ahead, joined by a rich crop of other talent. Schwantz's inside move at Hockenheim in 1991 to win by a hundredth is legendary ... he said it was unplanned – he'd just left his braking too late.

As corner speeds rose into the new century lines became more exacting, overtaking more difficult. The line between "safe" and "dangerous" was finer. It took Marc Marquez, up from bump-and-grind Moto2, to bring back aggressive moves.

1954

In the Heat

MALAYSIA DOES NOT HAVE A STRANGLEHOLD on heat, though nowhere can match the 1991 addition to the calendar's humidity. Heat waves can strike anywhere ... with some bad consequences.

The crucial accident at the Isle of Man TT that took the life of Spanish star Santiago Herrero was indirectly blamed on the heat of that baking summer of 1970: he had skidded on molten tarmac oozing up from the surface.

Climatic heat is complicated by engine heat: a factor in cases of exhaustion for riders sharing the enclosed space behind a dustbin fairing. It's still true with a normal fairing: MotoGP four-strokes shed prodigious quantities of heat, much of which lingers behind the fairing bubble.

Heat exhaustion is a factor, with one sidecar competitor needing to be resuscitated at Assen in the 1970s when his heart stopped after the race.

In Malaysia, it's endemic. Riders talk of how they sometimes suffer double vision as the race wears on. In 2010, Moto2 rider Scott Redding only just made it back to the pits before collapsing mid-race.

Right: Umberto Masetti, 500 World Champion in 1950 and 1952, strips to the waist at Assen in 1954.

Opposite: A giant fan is needed for Loris Capirossi as he waits with his wife Ingrid between practice sessions at the Malaysian GP at the Sepang circuit in 2009.

1957

In the Wet

FOR SOME RIDERS, rain is good news. In slippery conditions, the lucky few find an extra level.

All the greatest have been good in the wet; some outstanding. Multi-champion Jim Redman recalls his contemporary, 1961 champion Gary Hocking, as miraculous. "I asked him how. He replied: 'Ride exactly as in the dry, only smoother.'"

Rain is a great leveller, giving riders on lesser bikes a chance. Many one-time winners, including 250 riders Alan Carter in the 1970s and Australian Anthony West in the new century, benefited thus. Likewise Australian Chris Vermeulen, winning Suzuki's only MotoGP race of 2007.

It was simpler in the first 25 years: treaded tyres worked both wet and dry. However, the arrival of treadless slicks in the 1970s changed all that. Now if it rained, you needed different tyres or you would crash. After many problems, a flag-to-flag system was introduced, allowing riders to pit and change bikes.

TT schedules were often disrupted by fog. GPs hit some bumps: in 1989, the Belgian GP was restarted twice, then the second restart disallowed. Half points were awarded there, and at Shah Alam in Malaysia in 1995, for a 125 race flooded by a cloudburst.

It was nothing compared to 2008, when killer Hurricane Ike hit the inaugural Indianapolis GP. The 125 race was cut short, the 250s cancelled, and the MotoGP event red-flagged after regulation two-thirds distance. By then advertising hoardings and small tents were blowing across the back straight.

Left: A soggy start for Norton rider John Hartle in 1957.

Opposite: Even on special wet tyres, the streaming Sachsenring surface was treacherous in 2008. Dani Pedrosa (Honda, 2) will lead but crash; Casey Stoner (Ducati, 1) will win.

1963

Up in Flames

ONE ADVANTAGE OF A MOTORCYCLE compared to a car is that you are outside it. Should the 21 litres of unleaded gas go up, you can at least escape.

Usually, you have already left the scene. Bikes are not fire-prone unless they crash, then spill fuel into the trail of sparks. By then, the rider is already on his own.

It was not like that for Texan Colin Edwards at the Sachsenring in 2003. The filler cap of his three-cylinder Aprilia Cube had been left loose; fresh out of the pits he was hard on the brakes after the back straight: "I thought it was raining." But it was fuel, and with the exhaust backfiring gouts of flame, it went up.

Riding an exploding bomb, Edwards bravely abandoned ship at 100mph. He escaped injury and the bike cartwheeled to its cremation, leaving gouts of flame everywhere it touched down.

Occasionally, the consequences are much worse. East German refugee Ernst Degner took MZ's two-stroke secrets to Japan when he defected in 1961 and won Suzuki's first title in 1962. The next year, racing at the first Japanese GP, he crashed in the 250 race there and was left unconscious in a pool of burning fuel. Badly burned, he needed 50 skin grafts. Suzuka's double-right Degner Curves were named in his honour.

Left: A horrifying spectacle for fans at the Japanese GP at Suzuka in 1963: unconscious Ernst Degner is dragged badly burnt from the first-lap inferno. He survived, but required more than 50 skin grafts.

Opposite: Better fuel control in 2010 means the flames licking Randy de Puniet's Honda in Germany in 2010 will soon be put out. The rider is well clear.

1953

Race Message Boards

UNLIKE CAR RACING, ship-to-shore radios are banned in MotoGP. The only possible communication is via the pit board. And on the older longer circuits, perhaps another signaller on the far side.

The information needs to be simple, read at a glance. Generally in a race it is the gap between the man in front or behind, and in the latter case, his name.

In qualifying, it was a little more complicated: a rider was told his lap time (from the previous lap), as well as who was fastest and by how much. Nowadays each rider has an on-board lap-timer with instant read-out.

Pit boards have a further function: manipulating the figures can spur your rider on to greater efforts or bamboozle the opposition by displaying false instructions. Dani Pedrosa's team manager Alberto Puig is notorious for exaggerating the threat of following riders even when Dani has a comfortable lead.

The difficulty often lies in having time to see your pit board. At Rijeka in Yugoslavia in 1983, his pit was so placed that every time Eddie Lawson sped past he didn't see the big "Slow Down" signal or waving mechanics. He finished third, ahead of senior team-mate Kenny Roberts. It cost Kenny two points – the margin by which he lost the crown that year to Freddie Spencer.

Left: Only race position and remaining laps are shown to 125 rider Stefan Bradl in 2009.

Opposite: Read it if you can. No name codes in use at Monza's GP of Nations in 1953. Today Lorenzetti, Anderson and Agostini would be LOZ, AND and AGO.

1963

Refreshment

A RIDER CAN LOSE UP TO TWO LITRES OF FLUID in an average race ... more in the steamy heat of Malaysia. And certainly more back in the days of three-hour TT races.

At least TT riders had pit stops – and open-faced helmets – so they could, if they wanted take a slug of liquid while their bikes were being topped up. Few bothered.

The biomechanics of sporting effort are better understood today, along with the need to maintain fluid levels. Riders consume measured amounts of formulated energy drinks before the race, and often after it, under careful scrutiny of team physiotherapists.

One very enigmatic 125 and 250 champion of the early part of the century, San Marinan Manuel Poggiali, took the nutrition plan one stage further: taking a scale to breakfast in his hotel, then carefully measuring and logging the balance of protein and carbohydrates.

By then, Sete Gibernau had already pioneered a system used by a handful of riders today: an on-board refreshment bar in the form of a drinking tube connected to a water bottle in the hump on the back of his leathers.

Right: Casey Stoner's post-victory drink in Japan in 2010 is scientifically formulated and lactose-free.

Left: Mike Hailwood enjoys a drink following his victory in the 1963 Isle of Man TT, won while riding a MV Agusta at an average speed of 104.64mph.

1954

Pit Stops

REFUELLING PIT STOPS WERE A FEATURE of the longer road races of the early Championship years – at Ulster and the Isle of Man TT, where the practice survived until the World Championship moved on in 1977.

Engines were killed for the pit stops, with gravity-feed tanks topping the tanks while riders changed goggles and their machines were checked. They then had to perform another run-and-bump to get going again ... not always easy, with a hot engine.

After that, pit stops were confined to practice and qualifying sessions. Races lasting just 45 minutes were too intense for anyone who needed to stop to hope to make time up again.

The problem came with slick tyres in the 1970s: treadless rubber became unusable if it rained during a race, but a rider would pit to change tyres only if he really had no choice because GP bikes weren't designed with quick wheel changes in mind.

Races that turned wet had to be stopped and restarted. Then a solution was found in 2005 that reintroduced pit stops in a novel form. Instead of changing tyres, riders would change motorbikes, with their spare fitted with suitable tyres for the new conditions.

The rule has been invoked only now and then, but to the great enjoyment of all. Indeed the spectacle of riders charging into the pit and leaping from one bike to the other proved highly entertaining.

Left: Fergus Anderson bump-starts his 250 Moto Guzzi after a refuelling stop at the 1954 Isle of Man TT. Refuelling is banned in modern MotoGP.

Opposite: Some go-juice in practice for Loris Capirossi's Ducati in 2006. The only pit stops in modern MotoGP are to switch bikes if the weather changes mid-race.

1964

Controversy

YOU WOULDN'T EXPECT MOTORCYCLE RACERS to be angels. The raffish side is part of bike racing's character, especially in the early and middle years. Perhaps most surprising is that there haven't been more scandals over the years.

There have been plenty of driving bans – riders are notorious wreckers of rentacars. One (1984) 500 rider once boasted of destroying six in a year; an hotelier in Daytona erected a "No Parking" sign in the swimming pool. There have been messy romantic muddles, scrapes with the law after late-night partying and riders falling seriously foul of the tax man. There was even the case of the bomb in the brothel at the Macau GP in the early 1980s, but it wasn't a real bomb and it wasn't a real GP either.

The biggest real scandal involved 1981 World Champion Marco Lucchinelli. His riding career long over, he was arrested in 1991 and charged with cocaine trafficking. Pleading guilty to possession and admitting addiction, "Lucky" later described the three months behind bars as "useful", helping him conquer his craving.

Political controversy peaked in the 1980s, but you have to go back to 1955 for the start of it. Riders staged a sit-down strike on the grid at Assen over privateers' pay. Reigning champion Geoff Duke spoke up for them – and was handed a six-month riding ban as a result.

Right: Mike Hailwood twice missed court appearances in 1964 on charges of dangerous driving because of racing commitments abroad. He was arrested at the airport on his return. It cost him £100 in fines and costs.

Opposite: Italian Andrea Iannone and Spaniard Pol Espargaro (red leathers) get physical after a crash on the last corner cost both a chance of victory at Misano in 2009.

1965

Astonishing Feats

IN THIS LIST ONE NAME keeps on cropping up: Mike Hailwood. The British hero scored so many firsts in a relatively short career: first to win three TTs in a week. He also won three classes (250, 350, 500) five times in a weekend, twice on the same day.

Mike's greatest feat was at the 1965 TT. The Senior race was in bad weather and on the third of six laps, he fell at Sarah's Cottage, where new team-mate Agostini had crashed earlier. Bleeding from the nose, Mike kicked his MV Agusta straight, the screen broken off, restarted (illegally) against the track direction and continued to win the race, one of six Senior victories at the legendary circuit.

Geoff Duke certainly sustained a great feat throughout 1951, when his sharp and stylish riding on the simple but sweet-handling Norton meant he defeated the factory Gileras to win the title. The Italian bikes had 55 horsepower, the Norton just 40.

Margins have become tighter in the modern era. Perhaps Valentino Rossi's most astonishing feat came in response to a mere 10-second penalty for overtaking under the yellow (caution) flag in Australia in 2003. Smarting at a previous similar penalty and already champion, he got the signal on the 10th of 27 laps. From there to the end the Honda rider gave a virtuoso display of lapping on the limit, eventually overcoming the penalty and adding another five seconds on top.

Above: Valentino Rossi celebrates another humbling performance after beating not only his rivals (third-placed Nicky Hayden on the right) but also a 10-second penalty.

Left: Mike Hailwood inspects the damage to his battered and screenless MV Agusta after he crashed, remounted and won the Isle of Man Senior TT in 1965.

1979

The Waiting Game

OVER THE COURSE OF AN AVERAGE GRAND PRIX weekend, a racer of the 1950s would get at least six hours on his bike, spread over four days. Today, a MotoGP rider has just less than half of that: 90 minutes' practice, 20 minutes' warm-up and 45-odd minutes of racing.

A lot of the rest of the time is spent waiting: for practice or for the race to begin. Or for mechanics to get your bike ready to go out again. At least the modern riders have comfortable chairs.

Riders had their own way of dealing with the tension. There is a British tendency to laugh and joke around, shared by Mike Hailwood, Bill Ivy and Barry Sheene. Always there was the sense of something coiled tight within.

Other Latin types withdraw into themselves, becoming quiet and moody. Libero Liberati, 1957 World Champion, was notoriously even more taciturn before races. Today Rossi seems able to stay casual, until he draws the dividing line with his pre-riding ritual, starting off with twiddling his earring and finishing by standing on the pegs and pulling the seat of his leathers down on the pit exit road.

Kenny Roberts used to find somewhere quiet and lie down with his eyes closed, visualizing every inch of the lap, over and over.

Racing is a mind game as well as being a physical one. Using the waiting time is part of it.

Right: Spanish double 50cc World Champion Ricardo Tormo whiles away down time in the back of the team truck. The Valencia GP circuit is named in his honour.

Opposite: Tech 3 Yamaha rider Colin Edwards demonstrates his switch-off technique in 2010.

1971

Winning

WINNING IS EVERYTHING ... until the next time. If there is one lesson from racing history, it is that the present moves into the past, and the future takes over.

That's why the moment is so sweet; that's why it's necessary to savour it before it goes away.

And for that moment, it stays ever-fresh. Five-times champion Mick Doohan raced on more for "the instant gratification" of each race rather than the accumulating honours.

History also shows that riders from whichever era have a competitive spirit not shared by ordinary mortals. Perhaps it would be more honest to say that it is not the victory that counts as much as the fact that other people have been crushingly beaten.

Not just winning, but also how you win. And how and why the others lost.

In the 500 class Agostini's infinitely superior MV Agusta gave him seven years of winning by rote, and by miles. But in the 350 class, he was just as successful against much tougher opposition. Ask him about winning today, and it is those races he remembers.

Winning is like a drug. Get too much of it, and you only want more. This must be what drives 105-times race winner Valentino Rossi – approaching his late thirties and just as hungry as any teenager.

Left: A winning smile from Alberto Pagani after securing the Nations GP at Monza in 1971 for MV Agusta. His father Nello won the same race in 1949 on a Gilera.

Right: Emotion explodes over Nicky Hayden's face after winning the 2006 World Championship on the Repsol Honda. The battle with Rossi had gone to the wire, with Hayden on the back foot before the race.

1954

Losing

RIDERS TALK ABOUT the "Book of Excuses". It's something they need when they lose – a reason, some explanation. Something that they can improve on next time, so it won't happen that way again.

Losing always hurts, no matter how sportingly a second-placed man may congratulate his victor in public.

In the best cases, the excuse is to do with the motorcycle. Or the tyres. Each can pose insurmountable problems in a hard fight.

For the first 45 years of racing, the rider could even convince himself that there was some undiagnosed mechanical weakness to explain why the other guy rode away in front. In modern times, there's no place to hide.

On-board data-logging monitors both the rider and the machine. It records every movement of the throttle, every kiss of the brakes, every inch of every lap; it logs suspension movement and brake pressure, and prints it out in hard copy.

Even worse, if you lost to your team-mate, it can be overlaid with his: demonstrating how he was opening the throttle earlier and wider, and braking later.

Only the sinking feeling is left: that losing must be the result of the rider's own failings. It's an emotion hard to bear, and impossible to share.

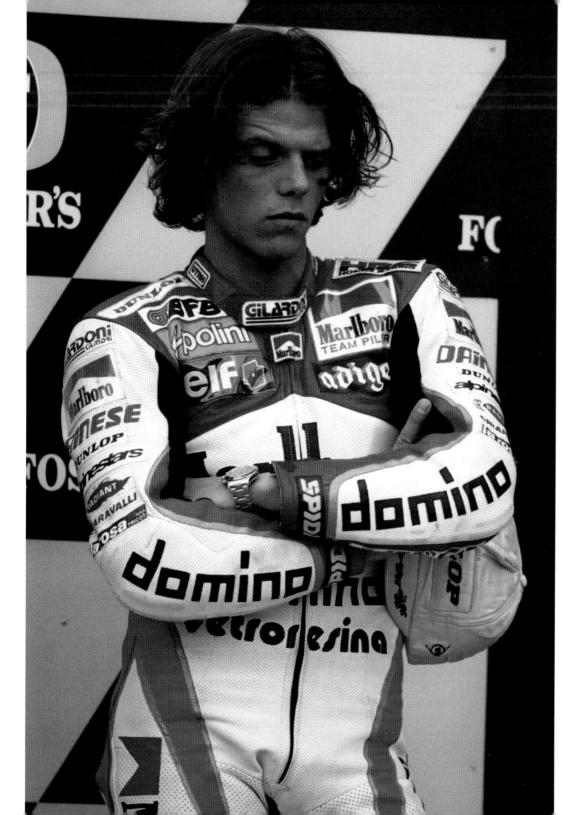

Left: Loris Capirossi was third, less than seven-tenths behind winner Max Biaggi and fellow-Italian Doriano Romboni, on 250s in Australia in 1994. His bitter disappointment is clear.

Opposite: MV Agusta rider Carlo Bandirola is the picture of dejection after being narrowly beaten back to third in the 1954 Dutch TT.

1954

The Chequered Flag

BLACK AND WHITE, instantly visible, instantly recognizable. An icon of motorsport the world over, the chequered flag is one thing that hasn't been replaced by lights or a computer.

It's how they finished races back in 1949, and it's just the same in 2011: the black-and-white symbol is waved for the winner and held stationary as the rest follow along.

As stationary as the flagman can manage. There's a tradition of over-exuberance, especially in the USA, at Daytona in 1964 and 1965, and in the late-1980s at Laguna.

Leaping around halfway across the track is discouraged in the modern era and only occasionally are celebrities given the honour ... like US TV's Jay Leno at Indianapolis in 2010.

The thrill of seeing it drop as he passes means the rider cares little about who is holding the stick.

The chequered flag also means the end of this book's journey, marrying old racing with new, past sights and sounds that prove so different, but have so much in common.

It will keep on waving in the future as well.

Above: The winner's wave. Dani Pedrosa passes the chequered flag after a gruelling wet French GP in 2013.

Left: The flagman cometh – this is what every rider dreams of seeing: the flag held aloft and dropped as he passes. This is Assen in 1954.

Picture Credits

The publishers would like to thank the following sources for their kind permission to reproduce the pictures in this book. The page numbers for each of the photographs are listed below, giving the page on which they appear in the book.

Action Images: /David W Cerny/Reuters: 33; /Kim Kyung-Hoon/Reuters: 25; /Simon Miles/Sporting Pictures: 35; /Mirrorpix: 18, 24; /Gustau Nacarino/Reuters: 115; / Tobias Schwarz/Reuters: 51; /Sporting Pictures: 13; /Mick Tsikas/Reuters: 43

Stuart Dent Archive: 6, 14, 16, 20, 26, 36, 38, 52, 58-59, 66, 68, 70, 74, 76, 80, 82, 84, 86, 92, 98, 106, 108, 110, 114, 116, 120, 126, 128, 132, 142, 146, 148, 156, 158, 160, 168, 170, 174, 178, 188, 190

faceCatcher.com: /Bernd Fischer: 2, 90-91, 166; /Gunter Geyler: 138, 150, 154

Getty Images: 96, 179; /AFP: 31, 151; /Bentley Archive/Popperfoto: 176; /Torsten Blackwood/AFP: 97; /Gabriel Bouys/AFP: 133; /David Caglio/FilmMagic: 29; / Stanley Chou: 107; /Michal Cizek/AFP: 95; /Chris Cole: 189; /Michael Cooper: 49, 125, 129; /Paul Crock/AFP: 161; /Mark Dadswell: 183; /Johannes Eisele/AFP: 149; / Express Newspapers: 78; /Bert Hardy: 30, 100; /Hulton Archive: 88; /Imagno: 72; /Darrell Ingham: 79; /Karim Jaafar/AFP: 5; /Jose Jordan/AFP: 167; /Keystone: 140; /Keystone/Hulton Archive: 162; /Saeed Khan/AFP: 169; /Dan Kitwood: 101; / Joe Klamar/AFP: 130-131; /Robert Laberge: 137; /Mirco Lazzari: 41, 69, 83, 89, 93, 105, 119, 123, 135, 139, 155, 164-165, 173, 181, 185; /Roger Lings/Keystone/Hulton Archive: 136; /Juan Mabromata/AFP: 37; /Luis Magan: 122; /Donald Miralle: 113; / Jean-Francois Monier/AFP: 191; /Don Morley: 184; /Kazuhiro Nogi/AFP: 177; /Peter Parks/AFP: 163; /Vincenzo Pinto/AFP: 143; /Popperfoto: 28, 46, 124, 134, 186; / Don Price/Fox Photos/Hulton Archive: 118; /Cristina Quicler/AFP: 19; /RacingOne/ ISC Archives: 10; /Jaime Reina/AFP: 27; /Miguel Riopa/AFP: 81; /Science & Society Picture Library: 144; /Andreas Solaro/AFP: 71; /Javier Soriano/AFP: 53, 57, 75; / Ronald Startup: 40, 44; /Harry Todd: 22; /Andrew Yates/AFP: 15, 23

Gold and Goose Photography: 17, 21, 64, 65, 87, 99, 103

JARROTTS.com: 60, 61

Press Association Images: 48, 56; /AP: 12, 32, 34, 50, 94, 112, 182; /ATP/DPA: 39, 77, 175; /Andreas Beil/AP: 47; /Manuel Bruque/AP: 187; /DPA: 127; /Peter Dejong/AP: 111; /Alessandro Della Valle/AP: 73; /Empics Sport: 104; /Armando Franca/AP: 117, 145; /Shizuo Kambayashi/AP: 11, 67, 147; /Jan-Peter Kasper/DPA: 157; /Ching Kien Huo/AP: 141; /Pius Koller/DPA: 153; /Ben Margot/AP: 121; /Daniel Ochoa de Olza/AP: 55, 109; /Jim Pringle/AP: 180; /S&G and Barratts: 42; /Alberto Saiz/AP: 85; /Hendrik Schmidt/DPA: 45; /Topham Picturepoint: 152, 192; /Eddie Worth/AP: 8-9

Private Collection: 63, 102, 172

Sutton Images: 159, 171

Topfoto.co.uk: 54; /National Motor Museum/HIP: 62

Every effort has been made to acknowledge correctly and contact the source and/ or copyright holder of each picture and Carlton Books Limited apologises for any unintentional errors or omissions that will be corrected in future editions of this book.

Right: The hero returns. British multi-champion Phil Read has just won the Junior TT on his Norton in 1961. He is greeted with a kiss from Maggie Sheene, older sister to Barry, in the checked shirt and cap.